Date Due

W Y15 Apr'48		
W X 280ct'48		

THERE I SQUANDERED MY SPARE TIME

BARBARY BO

A Story of the Barbary Pirates

BY

REGINALD WRIGHT KAUFFMAN

ILLUSTRATED BY
FRANK E. SCHOONOVER

THE HAMPTON PUBLISHING COMPANY
NEW YORK

CONTENTS

CONTENTS

BARBARY BO

CHAPTER I

GOVERNMENT GOLD

THE Consul thrust into my hands a huge double-barreled pistol.

"Now then, Martin," said he, "sit on the floor here in front of the coffer door with this — and don't go to sleep!"

Memory is a curious thing. When we get along in years and look back at our boyhood, certain important events seem words read in a book about another person, whereas happenings quite trivial shine with every color of reality and live again, as if they occurred no later than yesterday. So, coming now to tell of desperate

deeds I saw — and somewhat shared — among the
Pirates of High Barbary, I realize that much, and this
the most important part, will return to me only after
long summons; but other incidents, generally the lesser,
come running to mind, tails awag, like faithful hounds,
at the slightest whistle of desire. That is the way it is
with this, the start of it all: my superior often left me
in nocturnal charge of the office, and yet one occasion
stands out here, as you might say, right in front of my
very eyes:

The Spanish city of Cadiz, 17th September, 1803 —
a town of superb promenades along its harbor, and, behind them, quiet streets where no wheeled traffic passed
— a place of lofty, turreted buildings in Italian marble — of uniform houses glaringly white, flat-roofed,
Moorish. In from the evening Atlantic, a moist *viragon*
blew, carrying up our peninsula heavy odors of that
rotted seaweed heaped along the water-front; and I
stood in this ground-floor room of a house like all its
neighbors, except that, daytimes, it flew those Stars
and Stripes which are less than ten years older than myself; the American Consulate — I its somewhat im-

12

mature consular clerk.

"I don't see," thought I, "why Gonzales can't do this for once." I did not like Gonzales, and, as I then supposed without reason, did not, and could not, trust him.

Swarthy Ventura Gonzales, who called himself a Spaniard, lodged next door and had flattered Consul Wigglesworth's rather susceptible vanity until he got himself appointed Acting Vice Consul. The service was new and wretchedly understaffed, so that such employment of aliens was by no means extraordinary.

"Señor Gonzales," my superior continued, reprimanding my very thought by accentuating the señor, "has been given three months' leave of absence to visit Constantinople on private business. He left for Algeciras only a pair of hours since, while you were without doubt idling about the harbor."

The harbor was my mania — the harbor and ships and swimming. On the least excuse I always made for it, and tonight I was tired after an uncommonly long swim. My hours out depended largely upon Gonzales' hours in. Now, realizing all the favors that I must henceforth forego on account of his leave-of-absence, it was with a rueful smile that I said:

"Then there's no seeing the frigate sail — that American frigate which came in this noon."

Mr. Ahab Wigglesworth was gaunt and gray, with a face like a horse's.

"It's because of that pesky frigate you have got to stay here tonight. Those Naval sailors are without thought of consideration for others: they hauled the Government gold here after the banks closed. I am obliged to house it in our coffer until morning."

I looked dismally around the tightly shuttered, candle-lit apartment: a desk, shelves piled with dusty papers and calf-bound volumes on international law. The new coffer stood against the innermost wall. You must remember that Richard Scott's invention of a really fire-proof safe was then but a year old, and that, outside of London, scarce any wrought-iron ones existed; ours was a contrivance of cast-iron, and its vertical door opened to a key in the Consul's keeping.

Then, indeed, the episode became serious. The Consul and I were the sole people who slept in this

14

house, the appropriation from the United States being too meagre to hire corps of domestic servants, and our charwoman departing at each sunset. This evening, Mr. Wigglesworth was to be chief speaker at one of the mayor's eternal banquets, so here I must pass four or five dark hours as lone guardian of a fortune tempting to any of the thousand thieves in Cadiz. Tempting — for that coffer contained tribute!

It had long been the shameful custom of the greatest nations to send huge sums to the Barbary sultans, beys and pashas, rulers of buccaneering Morocco, Algiers, Tunis and Tripoli, in return for which those rulers would order their pirates not to molest ships of the generous country — until the money was spent, when another gift had to be given. Of course, everybody tried to pretend that these arrangements were "treaties"; as a matter of fact, however, the entire civilized world was paying tribute: it had too many troubles closer at hand to protect its commerce along the savage north coast of the Mediterranean. And, if the tribute failed, the pirates seized merchantmen, plundered them and held their crews in Mohammedan slavery for ransom.

America was not exempt — one of my own relatives, captured in '93 with the barque *President* of Philadelphia, Capt. Wm. Penrose, was held until our family privately bought his freedom — and even Mr. Thomas Jefferson had countenanced the "treaty-payments" because, he said, our land was "too weak for war."

Nevertheless, to war we had at last gone with one of the worst offenders: Tripoli; but this necessitated bribing the others into neutrality. Yusuf, the pasha of Tripoli, was a villain who had usurped the throne after exiling the rightful heir, his elder brother Hamet. Because our payments were delayed, Yusuf chopped down the Stars and Stripes and sent our Consul packing. We had to fight, whether weak or strong. Consequently, the Mediterranean was more dangerous for us than ever, and all our scanty shipping in those parts were needed for operations against the enemy. When there touched at Cadiz today a vessel bearing $20,000 intended to purchase the neutrality of Tunis, it was met by orders to leave its treasure with us until some boat could be spared to carry that gold to its destination, the original carrier meanwhile to join our

16

squadron designed for the punishment of Tripoli.

"So all that money's in there, sir?"

My weariness vanished as by magic, my all too round brown eyes must have goggled as I nodded toward the coffer.

"Martin Rowntree, it is not the money that irks me," Mr. Wigglesworth grumbled, drawing down the corners of his long lower lip: when he felt that the Government imposed on him, he would tell me anything. "They left a document, too. It's a secret memorandum to Hamet from Secretary of State Jim Madison."

A secret memorandum? My eyes must have begged for its contents. The Consul went on:

"Billy Eaton" — that had been our Consul at Tunis, banished last Spring by the Bey for his "distasteful remarks" about further presents from the United States — "Eaton has been at the Secretary, and this paper promises we'll support Hamet's claims to the crown of Tripoli if he will start a rebellion against his brother, Yusuf, our enemy. If that bit of sealed parchment fell into Yusuf's hands, sooner or later it would get to the European powers. You know as well

17

as do I, my lad, how jealous they are of us and one another, lest favoritism be gained in High Barbary. It would set them against us — it might make them Yusuf's allies. Seldom —"

"Cuck-koo — cuck-koo!" went the Swiss clock in the hall, eight times.

"Good Heavens, if I don't hurry, I'll be late for His Excellency's banquet!" The Consul adjusted his stock, pulled his cloak around him and started for the hall. "If I am, it will be the Government's fault. Don't you leave this room until I'm back! I've been about and bolted up everything. And don't dare to fall asleep!"

An instant later, the front door banged behind him. I heard him lock me in the house.

Always a gloomy place, the office had never seemed more so than now, when I was left here behind those fastened shutters and before a strong-box containing such wealth and such a secret as our coffer this night held. I was not a nervous fellow — for all my love of reading and study to master Spanish, I was strongly built, kept my body tough and had proved myself the

18

best swimmer of my age in Cadiz — but at this juncture I felt fairly jumpy.

The atmosphere of the room was like that of a narrow valley just before the advent of a thunderstorm. Moreover, although Mr. Wigglesworth, rehearsing his speech and carelessly enough passing the responsibility of the gold to me, had had at least the thoughtfulness to place a supply of fresh tapers on his desk, I — having left upstairs the book I was engaged upon, and having orders to remain at my post — found myself quite without congenial occupation.

Then I recalled the pocket copy of the New Testament which my father gave me when I left home, bidding me read a chapter nightly. Perhaps occasionally I forgot: here was a chance to make up. I put the big pistol in my belt, stood a candle on the floor and, sitting beside that illumination, with my head against the coffer's front, began where I had left off last evening, at the eleventh chapter of St. Paul's Second Epistle to the Corinthians:

"In journeying often, in perils of waters, in perils of robbers, in perils from my own nation . . . in perils in

19

the city . . . in perils in the sea . . . in perils from false brethren."

Little did I guess then how near was this to a catalogue of what the galloping future guarded for me, yet, at that word "robbers," my eyelids involuntarily twitched, and a mighty unpleasant tickle ran up my spine.

That office was the second room on your left as you entered the Consulate — a building situated within a stones throw of the hospital, the doric Casa de Misericordia — the first apartment being used as a general waiting-room. Our hall was wide and dark, with doors on both sides, and it ended in two flights of stairs: the first led gracefully upward, the second was of worn stone and plunged almost straight to a rabbit-warren of ancient cellars. Well, my chapter finished, I chose at random a volume of international law and reseated myself, my face turned toward the office's entrance, closed but not locked — there had never been a key to this since our occupancy — and the loud ticking of the Swiss clock clamoring through the crack above the sill.

"In peril of robbers!"

20

I tried to read — dull work.

"Robbers!"

I was really no coward. I thought of my Hempfield home and endeavored to recall the stirring adventures of my relatives now settled down there:

Colonel Nick Rowntree was younger than I when he braved Lord Baltimore's men in the Maryland Border War — about my age when he outwitted cross-eyed Van Veen, the spy, among the Indians at the seige of Louisburg. Detecting the Manor House Conspiracy against the Declaration of Independence, my twin cousins, Jeff and Stuart, were then somewhat my juniors: they later fought in the Revolution, and their father left the Continental Congress to join my father on the field of battle. [1]

What then of me?

During my earlier years I was a sensitive boy, with a fondness for out-of-doors, to be sure, but, mayhap, overmuch protected and coddled. My sole profound passion beyond books was — the sea. My ambition

[1] Martin refers to episodes for the most part narrated in the other volumes of this series, "The Rowntree Chronicles."

stood to join our still infantile Navy. This project, however, my surviving parent had opposed:

"You're not yet used enough to hard knocks," he had said, wanting to keep life still a little longer easy for me — and so secured me the Cadiz post.

What I loved about the place was the harbor. There I squandered all my spare hours. The smell of salt water, of tar — the natty officers — the tattooed sailor-men, some pigtailed, all bronzed, appearing from every unknown corner of the world — their yarns of sea-fights and legends of treasure-galleons — the sight of them shifting spars and bending and unbending sails — the daily picture of brig and frigate, full man-o'-war, felucca and the lateen-rigged xebecs from Africa: these were my daily joy, temptation and despair.

"Tick-tock — tick-tock," chirped that hall time-keeper.

I tried to read again; but, when fear was banished, wakefulness went with it. My eyelids grew heavy; I was very sleepy.

"Whereas Grotius, in his *De Jure Belli ac Pacis* . . . Pfendorf remarks . . ."

22

I'd been nodding!

This would never do. Dark — the candle had burned out. But I carried flint-and-steel: I renewed the light.

"Yet Liebnitz on the one hand, and Bynkerspoek
. . ."

I fell sound asleep.

I must have slid all the way on the floor and rolled some distance from the coffer, for thus I was when my eyes unclosed. I had dreamed of doubloons — it was the tinkle of gold that woke me.

On the instant, I was entirely conscious — and entirely alarmed, as well I had cause to be. A more disastrous tableau few can ever have been roused to regard.

Some draft from the hall sent high the shortened candle's flame as high as those of a miniature torch, and showed me — ruin. The door of our coffer hung open, a shiny new key protruding from its lock. Within, and lying on one side, so that the light revealed confusion, gaped a forced strong-box that could be none other than the box I had been left to guard. Much gold

23

remained in it, more lay scattered about me — one piece rolled lazily toward me as I looked — but not a sign of the precious document; save for the undisturbed, neatly tied files of the Consulate, there was not a trace of paper anywhere.

And what meant this draft? Another door was open — the door to the hall. With one motion, I turned and sprang upright! Yes, the back of a little, but mighty sinewy, man — money jingling in his wake and the Secretary of State's secret memorandum doubtless in his pocket — showed in swift retreat, at the threshold.

I reached for my pistol. It was gone.

Literally, I flung myself at him, and I went for him barehanded. He was appallingly rapid. I got but the end of his flying coat-tails, yet I got them in a vise.

He swung around. One of those tails tore loose in my left fist, and I fell a pace away. However, that which I saw would alone have sufficed to stagger me: the swarthy visage, the bared yellow teeth, the malevolent and flaming black eyes of Acting Vice Consul Ventura Gonzales.

He snapped a pistol in my face, belike the very wea-

24

pon Mr. Wigglesworth had given me. Something must have gone wrong with the priming, since a click was all my enemy got for his deadly endeavor. Still, so great a rogue was not to be stopped by such a small accident: ere I could close with him, he reversed the pistol and struck a murderous blow at my skull.

Perhaps I swerved. Anyhow, he must have thought me killed, as he had every right to, because he gave a single glance toward the front door and then rushed at the steps to the cellar; while I, having seen that, saw nothing else save myriads of stars darting across blackness. The blow had not landed where he aimed, but it came with enough force to fillip me back to the floor.

I bounded upright. There came two reports as of portals banged: the first, that of the stairs which led underground, the second, that opening from the street. I reeled forward — and almost into the arms of Consul Wigglesworth, his long cloak flapping, a reveller who had just returned from the banquet of the Mayor.

His glance surveyed wildly the speaking havoc of the office. His bony frame abruptly halted. Down fell his equine jaw.

"Hi! — Here! — What are you concocting? Explain yourself!"

And that other man, though of course Mr. Wigglesworth hadn't seen him, must be now somewhere in the cellar! I could not have answered had my life been the price of silence. I tried to pass the Consul and pursue.

"Stop!" he cried.

It was no time for obedience or explanation. He would have grappled with me — I thought, then, to detain me from danger. As he reached for me, I ducked — and he tripped over that book on international law which had already caused enough harm. He fell full length, his cloak entangling him. He had dined heavily, and had been long in poor health through failure to heed the warnings against the ordinary Cadiz water, which they collect in ill-smelling cisterns on their flat housetops.

Alarmed, I saw his cheek go from white to purple. Yet he would have surely stopped me had he been able instantly to rise.

Should I stop and help set him on his feet? Five minutes would inevitably be lost as a result in the

26

statements I should be obliged to make. He had to take second place in my attentions: the gold and the Government must have precedence. I snatched from him the pistol that he always carried and scuttled down to the labyrinthine cellars and the dark.

CHAPTER II

ACROSS THE MOUNTAINS OF THE NIGHT

THOUGH I had never liked Gonzales, I had never before suspected him capable of downright villainy. Now he had perforce revealed himself to my brief view in his real colors.

Of course he had learned, in the regular run of business, about the expected arrival of that gold and, after its arrival, about the dangerous memorandum accompanying it. Mr. Wigglesworth was a citizen whose patriotism was above reproach; his discretion was doubtful. He had certainly been as free of speech with Gonzales as with me, and it had never entered his trusting head to question his Vice Consul's loyalty.

Gonzales had been given a house-key when he came into our service. Probably long ago he secured a wax-impression of the coffer's key and had a duplicate made for use on the occasion when it would be most beneficial to him.

Well, here was the occasion! He invented some sudden call to Constantinople, pretended to leave, secretly returned and was at this instant making off with what treasure he could conveniently carry and with the far more valuable document, which he would vend to the highest bidder among my country's potential enemies.

I nearly fell down the steps as all this was suddenly clear to me. As I did so, I heard another door slam and realized Ventura's plan of retreat. He had heard Mr. Wigglesworth fumbling at the front entrance and knew as well as I that a second flight of stairs, at the rear of the cellar, led to the little consulate garden.

After him I leaped, bumping into some cumbersome obstacle — sprawling almost as flat as Mr. Wigglesworth himself on the hard dirt-floor, but picking myself up with better resiliency and hurtling on to those other steps. I dashed up them and reached the open. The *viragon* still continued, and there was no moon, but the dark blue of the heavens was heavy with discovering stars: there was my man already mounting the farthest wall.

I raised my pistol and levelled it at the sinewy sil-

29

houette of him. Before I could pull trigger, he was over
the top.

Not much ahead of me! I plumped down on the other
side of the stone barrier into an alley from which a
narrower alley led back to that street whereon the Consulate fronted.

Gonzales turned the corner. I turned it scarce twenty
yards behind him. I reached the otherwise empty
thoroughfare to see a saddled horse waiting — and
Ventura straddling it.

This time I fired. The shot thundered through the
silence; its echoes rattled down the sepulchral way.
The horse swayed, righted itself, fell; but its rider was
unhurt. He shook himself free and darted northward
afoot.

You would have thought I should bellow an alarm:
my anxious voice clove in my throat. You would have
supposed that the riot of my shot would raise the neigh-
borhood: at this epoch, brawls were too common in
Cadiz to drag householders out of doors — and far too
dangerous for onlookers to risk a head at an open win-
dow. No, Gonzales was speeding safely away. There

was nothing for me to do, if I were to recover that paper, but to speed in pursuit of him.

Up here and down there — around quick angles — through short-cuts and across wide plazas — we tore along. He had a brief lead and, although he did not increase it, my best efforts to diminish it availed me nothing. The white buildings ramped by, blind and uninterested. We met no patrol — we met nobody: Ventura knew the city and had the wit ready to employ his knowledge for the avoidance of company.

On we went — and on. There flashed across my mind Colonel Nick Rowntree's account of his race through nocturnal Boston — Cousin Jeff's encounter with the thief at "Lynton" [1] — there flashed a hundred hopes and despairs. Sometimes I felt sure I would somehow overtake my quarry and fight him for a hand-to-hand victory — sometimes, my breath slashing my lungs, I made as certain he would draw me into the mazes of the town's oldest portion and lose me there.

Neither of these things happened.

Doubling a dozen times, his course nevertheless quite

[1] See "Spanish Dollars" and "Seventy-Six."

consistently bore away from the city's centre. At the last wild tack, my outflung arm bashed against a wall, and my pistol was precipitated somewhere far to the left, in the darkness — unrecoverable. Yet this tack made plain Gonzales' purpose: he was definitely heading for open country.

Cadiz is a walled city. Which of its five gates would he attempt? He seemed to have for his goal the northernmost — but how could he hope to pass its guard? At our present rate of progress, continued in our present direction, that question must very shortly be answered. Straight beyond now the wall loomed, grimly forbidding in the silver light of the stars. The Vice Consul went right at it.

He chose no gate. The old ramparts were ill-kept and in disrepair. One stretch there proved to be — this stretch — where the top had fallen, and the crumbling sides proffered facile foothold. He evidently had counted upon it and even made his plans to come this way, though without pursuer. Not many minutes since he had gone over our garden-wall easily enough: this greater impediment he scaled with all the agility of a

32

gutter-cat.

Then I did let loose a shout; but the district was one of poor houses, in large part deserted. Nobody heard me, or, if anybody did, certainly no one heeded. Gonzales was safe across when I reached the spot whence he had begun his climb. With clutching hands that the stones dug into, and fuddled feet that missed every other projection, I, too, mounted to the top, hung one second over the farther side and dropped as lightly as I could to the ground.

Here the city ended abruptly, and a treeless sort of moorland rolled away to where, perhaps a mile distant, forest-land commenced. A faint path ran southeast, which must at last connect with a highway, and along this path the shadowy form of Gonzales was running. Should I follow any longer? I thought of my chief and could see him grumblingly stow the gold back into the coffer — what was left of it — still a-plenty for a temptation to robbers; but then I thought of Secretary Madison's paper. To turn back now would mean to lose the last hope of its recovery. No, I determined, however far this chase led me, I would go forward.

33

All across that moor I followed until the wilds opened before us — the wilds of the woods — and closed again. I followed, although near spent, to the highroad, and along it for perhaps ten minutes, the dense, leather-leaved *monte bajo* shrubs shutting me in, the Corsican pines blotting out the stars. A turn — and Gonzales was also blotted out. Where I hesitated, the vegetation somewhat lessened; but he was nowhere visible between me and the peaks massing upward to the Cerro de San Cristobal.

Dawn was coming, and with it came, from a short distance onward, a scent of cooking that reminded me of how hungry I was. Beside the road I presently spied a small caravan of gypsies encamped: four men they were, and two women who crouched around a fire a-crackle beneath a pot.

"Have you seen a man pass by here — a little, dark man, hurrying and out of breath?"

They crowded to me, smirking and curtseying. One of the women was for crossing her hand with silver and she would tell me a pretty future. As I shook my head, he who was evidently their leader, and whose name I soon learned was Silverio, pushed her brusquely aside — a black fellow himself, with a red kerchief around his head, hoop-earrings, a beak nose and ingratiating smile.

"Why, yes, young señor," he said, "we saw the person you inquire for. There is a fork in the road here, you see. Well, he turned full south down this prong of it, toward El Lago de la Janda."

Heavy of step, for I was dead weary by now, I turned that way, too.

The gypsy eyed me narrowly. "But will not the young señor break his fast with us?"

Mightily tempted, I told him I must hurry.

"We are baking hedgehog in the ashes, señor, and there is real coffee in the pot."

"I have no time. That man who passed — he robbed the United States Consulate at Cadiz last night, and I must catch him!"

"A thief? He carries gold upon his person?" Silverio's face lighted up; whether with envy or admiration, or something still else, I could not say, being convinced only that it was not horror of the crime.

"A good deal of gold," said I, knowing that I was not

35

far from the truth.

"And is there reward for his capture?"

The hint was obvious, and it suited me. With what I felt must be entirely veracious, I assured him: "The Consul will certainly pay well to recover what has been stolen."

"Ah, see, then: we are going that way. We shall help you. And we have our wagon and saddle-donkeys. We need not haste." Take at least a cup of coffee. I know every bush of this countryside. The thief cannot find a horse to buy. Come and eat tranquilly while my people harness the cattle. We have much time and shall lose none."

There was sound sense in this — and I was glad for guides and allies. Within five minutes, we were journeying, a crazy van behind me, containing the women and the man dismounted in my favor, I and the rest astride deep-saddled donkeys, tough little beasts with bells on their fringed bridles, led in from some hidden grazing-place nearby.

The gypsies soon found traces proving that Gonzales had forsaken the execrable highway for a worse course

36

ere reaching the one plantation at which he might have purchased a mount, and, as we pushed on after him, that course became worse and worse. The few farms dwindled, disappeared; more huts stood farther apart, then ceased altogether. Many tracks intersected, and the vagrants' skill at reading in the earth the progress of any predecessor — utterly unintelligible to me — would inform them that Ventura had turned now one way and again another.

"It seems uncommon queer," I ruminated. I wondered if I were doing the right thing. Yet what else could I do now?

"He wants to throw the señor off his scent," smiled Silverio.

"His best plan, since he must think me alone," I reasoned — I was very young —, "would have been to stop and fight me. The chances are even yet on his side, as far as he knows. He's a grown man, and I'm still a boy."

"Perhaps," suggested the gypsy, to whom I had told my whole story, excepting any word of the Secretary of State's memorandum — "perhaps he thinks to do

37

better than kill you."

"And what's better — for him?"

But to this question of mine, Silverio only shrugged, as if he meant something entirely obvious, or perhaps nothing at all. To me, there was no double meaning in that shrug.

We encountered almost nobody: none of those rural police who guard this district — I rather thought we made sundry detours to avoid them — but we did meet certain charcoal-burners and an illicit hunter or two, who would vaguely confirm my conductors' findings and report the fugitive always no farther ahead than could be accounted for by my hesitation at first loss of him and my later stop for coffee and a bit of crackling from the hedgehog.

"Why don't we gain on the fellow?" I demanded finally. "After all, he's afoot."

Silverio shrugged again.

"Can't we hurry?"

Said Silverio persuasively: "It is better not to come upon him till he is exhausted." And, as I could never have found my own way now, either backward or for-

38

ward, among all those twistings and turnings, I dared not forge on alone.

We rode deep into the afternoon, only an occasional word in Romany, which I could not understand, exchanged between my companions, and, save for that, no sound except the bells and the slow rhyme of our animals' hoofs against the clear Spanish air. I was increasingly puzzled by Ventura's strategy, and increasingly dissatisfied with my convoy.

About the gypsies, indeed, I recalled all the strange tales I had ever read or heard: how nobody knew whence they originated or what they were — how some said they descended from Hagar's son, Ishmael; others that they sprang from the man who forged the Golden Calf for the Children of Israel, and still more that they were first Egyptians caused to wander the world because their early parents refused shelter to the Holy Fugitives during the flight from Herod. On one thing alone did folk agree about them: that "their hand was against every man, and every man's hand against them."

It was nearing sunset when we came across a beggar,

39

who plodded from one distant city to some other, and he declared he had surely seen the man we sought as he went into a half-broken cart-road that rose, at one side, abruptly into thick forest-land, itself mounting toward a wooded and precipitous range.

Silverio, and a young fellow of about my own age, who was his nephew, examined the tracks and verified this statement.

"Your thief," said Silverio, wagging his head, "is crossing the Mountains of the Night."

Was he fabricating this?

He pointed to the range. I inquired where this course led.

"A short-cut," said he, "to Algeciras." — And he looked tremendously serious about it.

Algeciras! To be sure, that was his destination! There was no further question in my mind. We had better go on. Silverio's interest, I never doubted, was immediate money through the Consul; for me, only that I might put my fingers on that paper!

Up we climbed by that cart-track, and on upward for long hours. Night fell, but those vagabonds knew their

40

way, and I believe could see better by dark than at noon. The women probably managed to sleep in their bumping wagon; despite my qualms, I dozed on my donkey and nearly tumbled off him. Silverio rode ahead, singing softly:

> "Desgraciado de aquel que come
> Y bebe por manita ajena!"

From beginning to end, he sang that song over and over and over, nor between evening and morning would he heed what even I understood as his people's protests to pause for the preparation of a meal.

However, the slowest progress has the quickest end. I may have dozed more profoundly than at first, although I should have learned a lesson forever against such slumbers from my late experience before the coffer at the Consulate. Anyhow, my eyelids flew wide when my donkey stopped of itself because Silverio's had willingly halted just ahead and now stood there, barring the road.

The gray light that just precedes the sun bathed a wide landscape and seascape, and sent a fresh salt wind against our faces. We were at top of a small mountain; only low *monte bajo* growth surrounded us — on every

41

side the country fell away in gray gradations to the gate of the Mediterranean.

Although I had never been here before, I did not have to be told: there, below and across that strip of water already turning cobalt, rose Gibraltar's great Rock, English since 1783, with a clutter of spidery shipping at its foot, while, on the nearer side, were grouped the white roofs of Spanish Algeciras. Nor was this, for me, the half of my vision, because the road ran clear in front of us, and half-way down its length — entirely evident because no other pilgrim visibly trod it — trudged away from us a wiry little form that I should now have known anywhere: the fugitive Ventura Gonzales.

"Spurs!" I cried to Silverio. "There's the thief! Spurs — and after him!"

To my utter amazement, the gypsy blocked all advance. He shook his red-banded head until the hoop-earrings danced. He had drawn a wicked-looking knife from somewhere under his jacket, and, if he did not raise that weapon, his ingratiating smile was sufficient of a threat.

"Young señor," said he, "first you shall pay the poor, kind Romany their reward."

CHAPTER III

A WRONG ARREST

I T MUST have taken me a full five seconds to comprehend his colossal impudence — and my own real danger. Nevertheless, he meant exactly what he said; and, not only that, though it was improbable he would take the trouble and risk to kill me, he had it in his power certainly to detain me here until Gonzales should once more have disappeared.

"You are gone insane," said I, thinking hard for some way out of this.

Silverio's smile broadened until his hook-nose near touched his upper lip. He made a brief gesture to his subordinates, who were now only a few paces away from us.

"Then I'll go on alone," I vowed.

"Nor that, neither," said he — "not until I have some reward for my pains."

I looked anxiously about me. The other gypsies,

obedient to their leader's silent command, had closed in on every side, watchful and threatening.

"But," I persisted, "any reward there may be, will have to be paid by Consul Wigglesworth. I have no authority. Besides, don't you understand, it is not for sight of the thief, it is for his capture: you have not caught him, and you refuse to come along with me until I get him for myself."

Two quick phrases of explanation the rogue then did vouchsafe me:

"In the early morning there are often officers from the *aduana* along this road. They are armed, and they do not love the Romany."

From that I surmised that he and his band had had some trouble over a bit of smuggling, and from what everyone reported of Spanish jails, I could not wonder at this show of timidity. Still, my own affair, which was my Government's, pressed. I must not let it suffer because of these fellows' evil records.

"You haven't won the reward," I argued, fretting as the figure ahead put distance between us at every second lost in talk.

"We have guided you thus far, señor. We have guided you in the right direction."

That was true enough. I should never have got here without them. I should have been lost a score of times; yet part company with them now I must. A crude scheme toward escape began to formulate in my head. I dismounted slowly and, emptying my pockets of their stray coin into my two hands, advanced toward Silverio, who remained mounted:

"Then take this — it's all I've got."

It was not much: one gold piece, which I had been treasuring against fresh books, a few coins of silver and several odd coppers. He poked his nose forward to count them, and astonished disappointment flashed into his face. The other gypsies crowded beside him, peering in curiosity and avarice. Because I was attached to a Consulate, he had evidently serenely assumed that I carried enough to make this journey worth his while even if he could not overtake and rob the robber.

"You are concealing all but the tenth part, villain!" he bellowed, his face darkening even beyond its normal hue and his eyebrows lowering. He spat out something that must have been a Romany oath.

Whereat I acted. This had been my calculation: if those rascals were afraid of meeting customs-officers, the attention of such officers would not be invited by any shooting. I was therefore safe from any noisy death. What I must do was to get out of arms' reach and beat the donkeys, if they should give chase, down the descent until further following should become dangerous. So now, by an upward movement, I flung that loose money directly into Silverio's glum countenance.

He jerked back. His donkey reared and shook its bell-fringed head. I snapped around and sprinted at my topmost speed down the broad road toward the town of Algeciras.

Crude plans are really often the best, because they are so simple that your enemies count you too clever to try them. I have on several occasions won out by them, and this very day was to have to try out another. But their success generally depends on the surprise and rapidity of them. Silverio and his fellows came after

46

me for perhaps three hundred yards, the women shaking their fists at me from behind them; but they dared not come more — and, as I had surmised, did not attempt a single shot. Drinking in huge breaths of the salt air, I darted forward after Gonzales.

The wind was blowing inland from the water — that is, from the direction in which I was running — and yet he either heard me, or something else warned him. Perhaps it was the dusty clatter of the donkeys in so far as they pursued me, or the tinkle of their interminable bells — perhaps his guilty conscience told him that at this last minute someone for justice might have found his tortuous trail and be drawing near. Subsequent events that came all too soon supplied yet another supposition; but, be all that as it may, he looked back, observed me, seemed to recognize me — and set his nimble feet flying.

He had a splendid start this time, and made the most of it. On the other hand, in spite of my long hours with the gypsies, I was more excited than weary, and the muscles I needed for running had been rested somewhat. Man for man, I must now be in better condition than he.

So we coursed to the valley and on along the road across the brief plain.

, Even as I ran, my puzzlement remained with me. This grown person — I had had daily opportunity for long to observe him — was surely my superior in strength, for all that I was the larger: why did he not wait and kill me? There were as yet no witnesses to testify against him; there had been none night before last. What was it that forced him to convict himself by flight? He had fastened the cellar-door behind him ere ever Mr. Wigglesworth opened the front door. Did the thief suppose that, in the brief interval between then and my appearance in the garden, I found opportunity of revealing his identity? This would account for his not wanting to add a useless murder to the crime of robbery — but if I had named him to the Consul, Mr. Wigglesworth (so Ventura ought to reason) would have sent mounted help after me, and that would long ago have overtaken the fugitive and brought him back to Cadiz.

I could not make it out.

But I could run!

48

The sun rose with a quick, glad jump. The thick dust flew to right and left. The bushes brushed by. There lay the outskirts of the town — just ahead of Gonzales.

A group of shabby city-customs officers appeared, but they were having a heated dispute with a band of truck-farmers, whose laden carts were destined for the market. Gonzales had only to slacken pace the least mite in order to circle that miniature mob unobserved. He made the curve with a veritable swagger, almost egging me on to venture farther.

For my part, when I reached that group, if I had stopped to gain attention or assistance, it was clear that Ventura would have used the moments thus gained to become lost in the streets: the only sensible thing to do was to imitate his tactics. So, once around that noisy crowd, with their cabbages and cackling chickens, I bolted on after him into the not yet thoroughly awakened town.

It had already occurred to me that Gonzales might be seeking ultimate escape by means of a boat soon to sail for foreign parts, perhaps even impudently Constantinople, for which he had been given his leave of ab-

49

sence! Sure enough, the first conjecture was true, for
he now tore right for the waterfront. He reached it a
full half-minute before I did.

Good to see it was. I know this now as I look back
at that morning, though then no shaft of pleasure could
pierce my panting preoccupation. Quite six miles of
blue bay there were to the Rock, and ships riding there
— tall masts, delicate spars and jutting figure-heads —
merchantmen and men-o'-war; across that expanse, so
fine was this new day, it was possible to make out the
portlids and the gun-muzzles gleaming. The sunrise
cannon must have already sounded, although I had not
heard it, and — fresh broken-out, flapping in the gay
September breeze — flew the red banner of England and
the inspiring flag of my own country with its seven red
stripes and its six white, and the twinkling, reassuring
white stars in their blue field, which the Continental
Congress in '77 had called a new constellation. Hurried as I was, I wondered if the baby, Ohio, admitted in
February, had yet its 4th of July birthday present of a
star in this flag before me.

My true mind, to be sure, was kept to the nearer side

of the bay — the Algeciras side — and for Gonzales, making his final dash to its waters' edge. This proved wider awake than the town through which we had just run. Several of its boats, mostly Spanish or African by build, displayed full signs of life. One was about ready to sail, and her deck was swarming. Poor as the harborage is here, she had berthed close enough to fling a gangplank to the wharf-wall — and along that plank plainly well knowing what he was about, raced the miscreant Vice Consul.

"Hold him!" I fairly yelled, letting out all my lung-power. "Thief — *thief!*"

Not for nothing had I loved the sea and studied shipping. With a quick glance, I recognized that this craft, although she flew the British ensign, was an almost Oriental ketch, mounting some sort of guns. I saw that she was strongly constructed, but framed for speed — low cut, rakish. Her crew were distinctly busied with the canvas of her pair of masts — and she was square-rigged forward. I could even make out her very name, *Mastico* — it would be many a year before I forgot it! — in Roman lettering upon her prow. Yet I

51

had not paused to look. I panted unhesitatingly aboard not far behind Gonzales.

At once there formed a crowd of men around me, many more than those gypsies who had circled me on the hilltop, and far more terrifying. They were dark fellows with ebon beards and bare brown legs; denying the flag above them, Moors if ever there was one!

They surged to me. They crowded me across-deck to the farthest rail — they laid rough hands on me. And beyond them, peeping over their shoulders and shouting orders in a strange tongue that they obeyed almost automatically, stood the creature I had pursued through city and moorland and thence over the Mountains of the Night!

His swarthy brow dripped sweat down to his hairy chin; his chest heaved from his late exertions; his black eyes flamed hate — but they flamed triumph as well. More disconcerting than any menace, he disclosed his yellow teeth in a horrid grin.

I struggled and, for a moment, shook myself free. "That man's a thief!" I cried.

They laughed at me. In the jungles of their beards,

the teeth of all the men flashed.

Gonzales rushed to the land side; to the larboard side. He looked up and down the wharf and, making a trumpet of his hands, called:

"*Policia — policia!*"

The criminal was summoning the police! I could not understand that. But a moment more brought the explanation, for a squad of the Spanish harbor-patrol shuffled along nearly at once, bumptiously pushing aboard. Untidy, but formidable, they were; they had powder-horns swung from their belts, and they prodded these Moorish sailors aside with their carbines, treating them as if they were so many sacks of straw.

I was close enough to them to grasp the leader's arm. "This man, sir," I started, nodding at Ventura, "has stolen —"

His grin slowly contracting, the Vice Consul interrupted me.

"*Señor Official,*" said he, glibly, "I called you to take away this boy, because I have found him a stowaway upon the ship that, as luck would have it, is to take me to the city of Constantinople. He has been clerk at the

53

Consulate of the United States of America, in Cadiz. Two nights ago, he robbed the consular office, and it devolved upon me to apprehend him. Take him into custody."

Guess, if you can, my stupefaction!

Now at last I understood what cunning Silverio had surmised when his own crafty brain suggested that Gonzales might do better for himself than to kill me; now I understood why, instead of even attempting to murder me, thus ridding himself of my incriminating testimony, this fugitive had actually enticed me hither. For, enticed me he had, and I had strained every muscle to hurry into his trap.

He had easily conceived that when Mr. Wigglesworth found me alone before the looted coffer, I made off too quickly for explanation: the fact of no assistance coming after me demonstrated this. He even wanted me to wake up and give chase — at the last moment, when it would be too late quite to apprehend him! By inventing some plausible yarn about his return to Cadiz and subsequent departure — even changing places, as it were, with me and denouncing me as the pursued, himself as the pursuer — and by his present tale to these police — Ventura would clear himself of any suspicion, declaring that I had probably hidden the stolen gold and sold Secretary Madison's memorandum! Meanwhile, his nefarious work abroad accomplished, he would be free to return and begin fresh treasons.

Of a sudden, before me rose the picture of the poor Consul's face as I had last seen it. I dared not think of my father, who would never believe ill of me, but I saw that horror again cover Mr. Wigglesworth's horse-like features, and, for the first time, I thought that it betokened not only condemnation of the theft, but condemnation of me: perhaps he, even without Ventura's aid, already counted me guilty.

Pressing against that farther rail, besieged by unfriendly ruffians, I emitted a torrent of dismayed protest:

"He lies! This man lies! The truth is the other way about. Here stands the thief — look in his pockets! And he's running off!"

Gonzales calmly produced his credentials as Acting Vice Consul.

"This, gentleman, is *la prueba*," said he — and added to the "proof" what turned out to be a formal grant-of-leave from Mr. Wigglesworth, written on our consular parchment.

The Spaniards are great regarders of titles and official documents. The much moustached captain of the police-patrol squinted at these pieces of evidence. He pretended at least that — though I doubt if he understood a word of the text — he could read the English language. After an impressive silence during which he scowled at it, he drew back and respectfully saluted, handing back the document as if it were a treaty between nations.

Things looked black for me.

"I don't deny he's a Vice Consul, or that he has a leave of absence!" I stormed, near beside myself to view this plain case going against me and in favor of blackguard Ventura. "What I swear to you on my honor is that he is the thief. I tell you I followed him here all the way — and if you will but search him —"

Gonzales shrugged and raised his eyebrows significantly. "The lad confessed to me a minute since," he

56

purred. "Why should I summon you gentlemen, were I guilty? Now, at sight of you, he babbles absurdities. He is frightened by your powerful carbines, he is thinking — a few hours late — of the inconveniences of your jails. Unfortunately for him, these good fellows heard him confess."

Gonzales looked at the crew and said a few low-voiced foreign words. Confounded by such a colossal falsehood, I followed his gaze. It seemed impossible that he should not now have over-estimated his resources. At what I then saw my apprehension only soared: every Moorish head was bobbing assent to that outrageous deception.

"You did not hear me! I made no confession. I accused —"

There they stood, between Heaven's honest sky and Heaven's blue sea, impassive, utterly unresponding, merely listening as if struck into a polite attention. I tried again:

"You did not hear me! You didn't. You know I did not confess to anything, except to calling that man a thief. Oh," I cried, "isn't there a single trusty soul

57

among you?"

I appealed to them with every energy remaining, looking from one bearded face to another. In vain. As evilly-disposed a company of villains as sailed the Mediterranean, they gave me look for look, smiling their perjury.

"Señor," said Gonzales to the officer, "need we prolong this farce?"

The chief policeman laid a dirty hand on my quivering shoulder.

"What!" I protested in a final agony of despair. "Will you arrest me on the accusation of a robber backed up by a crew of unbelievers?"

That officer grinned. He had a swarthy, twisted face, and the end of one side of his *moustachios* was tilted a full inch above the other, giving him an added ferocity of expression: he looked all gloating satisfaction.

Then, indeed, speech failed me. Nay, I knew no words could help. A child could have seen that to think the worst was this scamp's nature, and that to inflict pain was, as with so many Latins, his pleasure.

"I arrest you," said he pompously, "on the accusation of no crew of unbelievers and no robber. I arrest you on the accusation of the Señor American Vice Consul of Cadiz."

CHAPTER IV

UNDER WATER

THE policeman's hand was on my shoulder. His fellow-constables were ranged in front of me. At either side crouched a crew of murderous Moors headed by this traitor Gonzales, whose lips were still black with the false accusation that all the surrounding company either lyingly supported or eagerly received.

Could any human course help me? That farther rail was against my back. I felt its pressure as I cowered fast against it, and the touch of the insensate wood sent a mad idea hurtling up to my fuddled head.

Open water lay there, directly below. If I could gain it — It would mean death if I missed —

The captain of the guard frowned, about to seize me.

I gripped the rail with both hands — flung high my heels — turned a back-somersault and shot headlong into the azure of Algeciras harbor.

There came a deafening splash that shut out the shouts and confusion which, on deck, must have succeeded my wild act; there came, too — and instantly — the numbing shock of cold water, for the sub-tropical sun had not yet warmed it. Down I went into its depths, and still on down. My ears thundered; it seemed as if my ribs and lungs must be crushed by the enormous weight thus put upon them; yet fear of being shot at when I rose overcame the natural desire to struggle too soon toward the surface.

Still downward!

Would they shoot? Would they dive after me? Would they put out a boat?

That harbor, as I have said, is comparatively shallow. I had near reached bottom before I struck the level at which the density first stopped me and then began to lift me upwards. I fought it one moment; the next, common sense partially returned, and I struck out under water in what I assumed to be a course away from the *Mastico*. As long as I could I kept below; when I was forced up at last, a turn of my head showed me the ketch forty-odd yards behind.

61

My enemies were ranged cheek by jowl at the rail. Somebody — Gonzales, I guessed it to be — snatched a policeman's carbine and fired.

Simultaneous with that spurt of flame, in fact, as the bullet struck not far from my head, I dove again and again began to swim under water. Lucky it was I had made myself an expert! This time I kept below longer than ever my most ambitious dreams had pictured it possible.

Whether those people on the *Mastico* thought me hit and done for, it is impossible to tell, but when far advanced suffocation brought me back to air, I saw her rail deserted. The crew were at work heaving round a capstan; the patrol, returned ashore, were running along the beach. The ketch appeared more anxious of a sudden to make sail than to verify my demise, and the police, if they saw me, probably concluded that I must soon strike for solid earth, when they could affect an easy capture. Nobody seemed to suppose a lad would attempt those six miles across the bay to British territory.

Nevertheless, that was what I had in my mind to try,

seeing no other course, and I set out with all my strength and caution, for, Gibraltar gained, the terrors of a Spanish jail would be at least temporarily over. I husbanded my forces and plodded forward with the great Rock for goal.

As soon as I dared, I rid myself of boots and jacket. I changed my stroke frequently; when past the middle of the bay, I rested myself by floating. But it was a hard pull, and there were minutes when it looked as though the swimmer would never reach his destination. Exhaustion crept upon me, and I had been none too fresh at the start. My muscles responded more and more stiffly to my will; sight began to fail as I drew near some of those big ships which I had seen from the hilltop; I found myself trying to circle one when an icy cramp seized my left leg.

Unless something happened, and that speedily, this meant the end of me. Spluttering, all sound choked out of me, I looked crazily upward, and could not see the deck — only the vessel's vast sides towering, perpendicular, heavenwards.

Only those vast sides without promise? Why, here —

I wasn't out of my head. Here dangled a rope-and-wood ladder, from that ship's upper regions. It hung for the convenience of some longboat sent to establish shore-communication. The lowest cross-bar was just overhead.

I raised myself as far out of the water as was possible. I touched the thing — and no sooner touched than clung fast to it for dear life. Rung by rung I drew myself up.

As soon as I got clear of the water, the cramp left me; but my strength had been sorely strained. As the first wide port came abreast, force failed and will weakened. I tumbled into that opened mouth — fell — rolled over — and lay like a lad beyond human aid.

CHAPTER V

STOWAWAY

WHEN my normal intellects reasserted themselves, they bore two new alarms. From somewhere overhead trampled heavily shod feet; blocks creaked; ropes ran over sheaves; the gurgle of water was audible: the vessel was under sail. I observed a long table set with tin plates and pannikins; twin rows of sailors' bags and sea-chests were about; arm-racks around the stanchions, bearing cutlasses, muskets and long, double-barrelled pistols: this was the mess-deck of some ship-of-war!

A step lumbered toward me. Having fallen between a pair of boxes, I made myself as small as I could and shut my eyes. There was not any reason to it — just instinct. Nor did it, even for that moment, save me.

"Hello!" — That was a thin, but raucous, voice. As its owner bent, I caught a whiff of soured rum. "Here's somebody hove down for a full due," it went on, and in my own language.

The toe of a big boot thrust at my ribs through my water-soaked shirt, and none too kindly. I lay mighty still.

"A boy, at that," the voice went on. "Hi-you don't belong aboard o' us. Stir your stumps, or I'll h'ist you through this port in a brace o' shakes!"

The boot became cruelly insistent. I had to look up at a figure sinister enough in any circumstances and wickedly antagonistic now.

Enormous Gustavus Wilson, called "Gus" — I was soon enough to learn the name he gave himself, although it could hardly have been his real one! — bore about him no marks of nationality. He spoke English sometimes like one of us, but often like an Englishman, which is not uncommon with seafaring folk, who pick up fresh twists of tongue at so many ports. He was as much bigger than I as I was than Gonzales, and he was correspondingly powerful: never have I seen such arms or such depth of torso. He had blue eyes, fair skin, light hair — always towsled. His expression was one of nasty craft that directed his mere-brute face; his glance

66

glowered; his lips perpetually sneered above blackened teeth, and — no fault of his own, yet it added to his air of malignity — his right shoulder was a good three inches higher than its mate.

"Well," he rasped, "will you know me the next time, mister?"

I had been blinking at him, as was my habit when doubtful or nervous: how often I had been corrected for this at home! My apology doubtless rang falsely enough.

"Nice bit o' play-actin' you're tryin' to give me," he interrupted.

"If you please —" I began again.

"Shut up!" he screeched, and his voice was the more terrifying because it was that of a miniature devil in the body of a deformed Goliath. "Get up on your feet and explain to me respectful' what it is you're doing here."

He grabbed my left ear with an agonizing twist, and so jerked me upright. Between my rapidly rising and falling eyelids, tears involuntarily, but insistently, welled.

"You blubbering ninny!" he scraped out. "I believe

you're a girl."

Well, that was too much. I somehow tore out of his grip. Of course it was his duty to report me, but there was no need for torture: at risk of leaving an ear in custody of his pinching thumb and forefinger, I jumped away.

He sprang after. My flying hand encountered an arms-rack and a cutlass. I had the bare blade free and raised before he — or I, for that matter — knew what I was about.

"If you — touch me again —" I panted.

Then and there I learned my primary lesson in what desperation will do toward overcoming a bully: instead of attempting to disarm me, he fair flew backwards. He put the mess-table between us. The easy sneer froze on his lips.

"I'll — I'll call the crew!" he yelped.

"Do," said I. My spirits rose with his retreat. Any officer's severity must be juster than the savagery of this underling. "Then they'll bring your captain. I won't have any truck with your sort."

It was big talk, but it did not calm him. To summon

help, he actually cupped a palm around his mouth. But he didn't shout. Too soon for that, up behind him rolled another shape; a hand drew his bent arm down, and a low drawl demanded:

"Now, now, Gus, can't you ever pick anybody your own size, hey?"

Beside my enemy stood a man of about fifty, having a weatherbeaten face and eyes of the sort you know at once have fronted all the perils of the Seven Seas and feared none, taking them as the come-and-go of life. His tarry pigtail showed first over one shoulder, and then over the other, as he wagged his head. In different circumstances, he might have appeared scarce more prepossessing than his fellow, for the newcomer's nose had been broken in some fight — honorable or otherwise — and never rightly set, while a red scar across his forehead drew an eyebrow crooked at the corner; but he was against Goliath, which made him welcome to me.

Moreover, Goliath further quailed at sight of him. "Let me go, Bill Ray! Look at his cutlass. A stowaway!"

It was the second time today that I had been thus

described; but now at least I was on a craft whose crew, by their speech, were either Americans or English. I pinned my faith on the man addressed as Ray.

Without loosening his hold of the big chap, this Ray bent across the table toward me. I saw he wore silver finger-rings, such as they sell in Spanish ports to visiting mariners, and he had brass circles in his ears, very like the gypsy Silverio's. He said to me, in a conciliating manner:

"Now, then, hearty, don't you think you'd better stop fighting my poor, little friend here and tell me what it is ails you?"

My weapon dropped. I went hot in the face, but I did not let go my resolve.

"There's only one man aboard has a right to question me," I declared stubbornly; "and he's the skipper. Take me to him."

A broad grin sent ripples over Ray's red face the way the wake of a boat disturbs quiet waters. "I likes your courage, my hearty," said he.

His neighbor only scowled:

"There'll be James McKenna to pay for these here

doin's yet."

"Never you mind." — His phrase being new to me, I assumed it to refer, in some manner, to the ship's commander. — "Captain McKenna will be my affair."

Bill Ray broke into a roar of laughter. "The boy don't know!" He clapped me between the shoulder blades. "That earns it!" he vowed, his scarred eyebrow tilting still more crookedly. "That speech earns it. Come along."

I was thoroughly mystified. He wheeled and started to roll away. Wilson, if he turned a sullen back, at least offered no objection. I followed Ray, leaving the discomfited one behind.

My journey wasn't long, and, though frightened and tired, I managed to keep my head high while the strange faces of the crew peered at me, wondering. We passed through a dark corridor, thence, deviously, to the main deck.

The shore was already vanishing, the Rock a blue cloud against the horizon. I was aboard a frigate, two-thirds of her canvas set before a spanking off-shore breeze, and her sailors busied, no longer in uniform, but in messy sea-clothes. Ray nodded to a pair of officers in talk a few paces forward, the nearer a very young person with a square jaw too old for him, the other spectacled and somewhat his elder.

"No, my hearty," said Bill, "I can't go much further with you, but if you'll just keep up the courage you showed Gus Wilson yonder, you'll come to no great harm, I'm thinkin' — addin' a pinch o' salt o' respectfulness, hey? Only, they's one hint I'll give you 'fore I turn you over to Lieutenant Porter — him that's conversin' with Surgeon's Mate Cowdery over there."

Somehow no longer so anxious to meet officials once I was above decks, "Yes," I answered meekly enough: "what hint?"

"Why, this, and no more. To say there'll be James McKenna to pay is a mere manner o' speakin', which means they'll be trouble, which there needn't be in your case. The commander of the U.S. Frigate *Philadelphia* ain't any McKenna, thank your stars; he's Cap'n William Bainbridge. We carries thirty-six guns. We'll soon be joined by Lieutenant Smith's schooner the *Vixen*, mannin' twelve eighteen-poun' carronades and a

72

pair o' long 'uns — and it's an open secret how our orders is, after holdin' up any and all hostile vessels encountered on our course, to *proceed* to Tripoli and blockade her! You're goin' to war, my son. That's where you're goin'."

Ray gave me such a shove with this that I felt the war must be pretty near at hand. I all but fell at the feet of the officer to whom he straightway assigned me.

"Stowaway, sir," announced Bill, cheerfully, dabbing at his forelock as an excuse for a proper salute. He half-revolved on his heels. That was the last I saw of him for many an hour.

Near out of my wits by now, what with adventures and advice, I yet risked looking about. In his turn, Dr. Cowdery studied me through his steel-rimmed spectacles as if I might be some rare specimen of sea-creature, washed on deck; but the Lieutenant gave me only the briefest glance, which I repaid with compound interest. This, then, was David Porter. His fame had reached our Consulate as the prize-crew's master of Reis Mahomet Sons' pirate-polacca — as originator of last May's reconnaissance in the port of Old Tripoli and

73

burner of the enemy's craft there under the enemy's shore-guns — yet in years he seemed not much more than just my senior!

"Sir —" I started, and tried awkwardly to salute a little better than Bill.

"Follow me," Porter ordered.

Stowaways, it was clear, were nothing unusual in his wide experience, but pleas from them were both unusual and dangerous. Cowdery good-naturedly enforced this supposition by smiling at me encouragingly and putting a long finger to his thin lips.

I was shown into a combination of office and state-room and left face-to-face across a desk from a personage whom Porter had addressed merely with a formal "Sir." I had once seen this man from a distance in Cadiz; I recognized him at once to be no less than Captain William Bainbridge.

"What's this — what's this?" — That question, thus querulously repeated, constituted the first words I ever heard from him.

In those times, the whole world smiled at our young Navy, even our land-folks back home, most of whom thought we ought to hire Naval services from stronger nations instead of wasting tax-payers' good money on anything so unnecessary. What we had of a Navy, therefore, was consequently anxious to make its lasting reputation, if only with such ships as Commodore Preble's "Constitution," which was generally derisively referred to as "a bunch of pine boards." Badly fitted out and only half manned, the four ships in the Mediterranean had an almost impossible task before them. A youthful service, our Navy was the place for youths, but Preble complained of the men under him that he had been given only schoolboys for officers, every one of them being less than thirty years of age.

Bainbridge, like Porter, was a case in point.

He was, I knew, a thorough sailor and an excellent commander, having followed the sea, first on a merchantman, since he was fifteen; but, try though he severely did to look and act older, he was just twenty-nine, and not all his efforts could add a day to his appearance. Here he sat glaring at me with the stare of an antiquated admiral, in a blue coat with great brass buttons and gilt facings and epaulettes, his throat

buried in a stupendous high collar, cut open to display
the stock below his chin, and the rest simply long nose,
side-whiskers and a curling head of hair rising upright
to what most resembled the comb of an angry game-
cock.

"What's this? — Aboard o' me? — Stowaway aboard
o' me?" he bellowed.

However they might seem to the departed lieutenant,
this belligerent Captain evidently intended me to know
that he considered stowaways little less culpable than
traitors — and for my part, I was now about as sick of
them as he was! Anyhow, he half jumped from his
chair as he thumped on his desk.

I blinked — but he still looked only twenty-nine.

"Yes, sir," said I — "technically."

It must have been three years — or since he won his
present rank — that anybody had talked to him like
this. My words were spontaneous — discipline always
came hard to me — but they brought him erect.

"Technically?" he repeated. "How the deuce do
you dare quibble with me?" His whiskers bristled, his
nose twitched; he let out such a broadside of I dare say

justifiable abuse as might have staggered anybody. "Explain yourself, and then get ready to be put in irons! Go on: you may speak your own Spanish — I can understand you!"

It might have frightened anybody; but there are limits to fright, and I had this day reached mine. These things are cumulative. The crime of Gonzales — the pursuit across the Mountains of the Night — the narrow escape from police and Moors — my exhausting swim — Wilson's threats and would-be torture: upon my word, I scarce cared, at this end of it, what was done to me by the boyish Captain of the *Philadelphia* — for that it was — be he never so powerful. I didn't remember Bill Ray's advice about courage: there was none left in me except the courage of not caring; I was just too tired to think.

"I can speak English," said I, "for I am an American citizen born. I am — or was — American consular-clerk at Cadiz. The Vice Consul robbed our safe of money and a secret paper from Secretary Madison. At least, the Vice Consul says I did, and I know he did. But I'll tell you this: he's aboard a ketch — the *Mastico*

77

— manned by Tripolitans, for all they pretend not to be, and fly the British flag, and the *Mastico* put to sea from Algeciras this morning. If you'll catch that ketch, or put back and turn me over to Americans at Gib — not Spanish ones at Alge —"

Despite my lackadaisicalness, it was one of the longest speeches I had ever made, yet it was interrupted. Captain Bainbridge jumped around his desk at me and shook me until my teeth chattered like the castanets I used to hear ashore.

"I gave you a chance to explain — explain — and what do you do? Insult an officer of the American Navy with a cock-and-bull yarn like this! Go out of my course to overhaul a mythical Vice Consul turned thief? Put back to port for the sake of a stowaway who's lost his wits? Why, you nameless wharf-rat —"

He was on the point of calling the officer-of-the-deck and having me locked up: I saw thus much. I understood, too, that he had stopped only because anger choked him. So, remembering a fellow's debt to his family, I decided I might as well hang for a sheep as a lamb.

"Throw me into irons if you want to, sir," said I wearily; "but don't call me nameless. The Rowntrees of Pennsylvania are every bit as good folk as the Bainbridges of New Jersey."

Little could anyone have guessed the effect of this. He released me so suddenly that I near fell backwards. The skipper of that frigate gaped at me.

"Rowntree?" he echoed. "From Pennsylvania? You don't mean to stand here in those rags in my cabin and tell me you chance to be kin of Congressman Frank Rowntree?"

They were rags by now, and wet and miserable and unkempt as I was, I must have looked disreputable. Now it was exactly as if a new dawn was breaking. "Sir," said I, "though he is a much older person than I am — or than you are, for that — Mr. Frank Rowntree is own cousin to me."

The Captain seized me again, but now in a very different fashion. He pushed his broad face close to mine, his nose seeming longer than ever, and his bright eyes searched my eyes.

"Boy," he demanded, "can you prove that under a

79

bit of cross-examination? Why, Congressman Frank Rowntree it was who chiefly supported my own Congressman in getting me out of the merchant-service and into the Navy as a lieutenant in '98!"

80

CHAPTER VI

THE PIRATE FLAG

SO IT happened that I, who had entered Bainbridge's stateroom as a lieutenant's prisoner came out of it as a captain's cabin boy:

"Your good-for-nothing predecessor deserted at Gib," growled the commander, "chicken-hearted at our last landstop before Tripoli." But the growl was not dangerous, though the Captain shook his head till his curly hair tossed like a ship in a storm. "I need a cabin boy, anyhow. It's dashed irregular, but I can't do less for even a harum-scarum member of the family of a man who did so much for me. You ran away from dry-as-dust Wigglesworth — oh, I know him! — to join the Navy. Well, here's your chance."

Thus, in his character of skeptical old salt, the young Bainbridge insisted on viewing my case. Although I tried to convince him of the truth, his brusque good nature ordered silence, and obedience became obligatory. Once I admitted my long-standing ambition to follow the sea, he saw his way out of a difficulty by believing — or pretending to believe — that all the rest of my story was a pack of fables concocted to gain this end.

"Not a word more of that," said he — "not a word about vice consuls turned thieves and Tripolitan boats flying false colors. Of course, you know your offer to prove your tale by having me go out of my course, or put back to port, was impossible, and it was clever enough of you — clever enough. But we've plenty of serious work ahead of us, with little enough equipment for success, without looking for foolish trouble even if it's half way true. When we go back, I'll try to explain your French-leave to Wigglesworth and the State Department — and your own people. Only, favoritism is over now. I'll have you instructed in your duties."

They were light enough, as it proved, and of brief duration each day. It suffices that I performed them satisfactorily enough until the fatal day that ended our expedition. What turned out more important to my future was this: during our cruise — for we went none too fast after the *Vixen* joined us, and we touched at both Malaga with its vineyards and Malta with its fortifications — my leisure found a master who taught me the rudiments of seamanship: Billy Ray, broken-nosed and pigtailed veteran. Wilson I generally managed to avoid, except to encounter occasionally a malignant sneer from him across-deck, which boded ill, but Bill took me under his special protection and put me straightway to school.

He pointed out the beauties of the frigate's construction, going into minute details; he explained everything which my avid reading at home, without actual illustration, and my zealous observations along the Cadiz quays had left me in the dark about; he saved me many a tickling from the bo'sun's rope-end. The *Philadelphia* was running upon formal card — watches of four hours on and as many off — so time was not lacking.

"Never fear — do what you're told — and do it as neat as pie, my hearty," he would over and over again drone to me: "that's the secret of a happy mariner's life — hey?"

An indefatigable man he was. It was no time before he had made me able to box the compass and understand the flag-signal code; as soon as I could tie any nautical knot — reef, bowline, figure-of-eight, Carrick bend and swab-hitch — I was instructed in pointing a rope; when this style of plaiting came easy, I received the theory of steering, and when I had mastered that to some degree, Ray went into infinite lectures concerning the setting and furling of sails. With our Navy so juvenile, though there existed discipline, it was one day severe and the next day haphazard, and, since we had sail-drill each forenoon, I was given a chance to go aloft. Well do I remember my first giddy sickness with the frigate swaying now to this side, now to that, and my final exultation at overcoming it.

"They that go down to the sea in ships" acquire more than ship-wisdom — all in all, here was a not unhappy cruise for Martin Rowntree. I had, indeed, only a single real discomfort, for I was too young to worry my head over the physical inconveniences. My concern was the traitorous Vice Consul who had escaped and carried with him that perhaps fatal letter of

84

Secretary Madison! Still, with the Mediterranean a warm and lazy blue, or with the golden, low-lying stars for our only company, it was easy to postpone, at least, land-complications; besides, our commander had shut off all complaints on this score; but you may be sure that I thought not a little about the results of my unfortunate napping in the shadowy house in Cadiz, and laid a hundred futile plans. On more than one night I dreamed of somehow seeking and finding Ventura Gonzales before he could dispose of his stolen document.

In such-wise, matters continued until we almost reached Tripoli, when the *Vixen* got orders to lay-to while we, going forward alone, should make the necessary reconnaissance. The *Philadelphia* ploughed steadily toward the enemy's headquarters.

It was the last day of October: if you have not done so already, set it down on the tables of your memory as momentous in American annals. We had had, recently, a spell of rough weather, but this morn broke fine, with a brisk in-shore breeze blowing and the sea running light. I came on deck to see the sun shine clear over the near water and the far-off land. No great time was consumed for our consort to drop completely out of sight behind us. Before us the gray-green coast peeped over the Mediterranean's edge.

Eight-bells it was. I was officially off duty and inching as far forward as I durst go, to view the coming end of our journey. "Death before Tribute": how often had I heard that toast, before ever I had come to Cadiz! Were we going to be able to back it up?

Already I could see — just see — the flat roofs of Tripoli's white houses, so much lower and more uniform than those of Cadiz — the ships in front of them — the shining minarets of mosques. From where I was, it seemed a wonder-city. Our crew were all at stations, Bainbridge, with Lieutenant Porter beside him, at his proper point of vantage, a spy-glass under one arm.

Two-bells! We were scarce seven miles off-shore.

From above a distinct call rang out. It descended from the lookout in our crows nest.

"Sail-ho — two points off the starboard bow!"

I looked. It seemed incredible I had failed to note it sooner. There it was, plain as a pikestaff: an unmistakable craft of some sort, not so far in-shore from us and

86

standing taut before the stiff breeze to westward.

Nothing really remarkable about that; but we had come as blockaders, and, for my part, I stared at this apparition, her lines becoming more and more familiar. She was a ketch. It was not only that the wish was father to the thought: she was —

Gonzales and the Secretary's letter: my dreams were coming true! Since we had sailed up with her, the robber had surely not yet found a chance to negotiate his sale.

I ran boldly right up to Captain Bainbridge. How my breath died — how my brown eyes danced!

"Sir," I blurted it out, fighting for a calm manner, but knowing full well that my face was unwarrantably red, as ever was the case when I was excited, "I'm sure of that boat. She's the one I told you about — the one that ran away from Algeciras: she's the *Mastico*. Ventura Gonzales is aboard her, our renegade Vice Consul from —"

The Captain lowered his glass and faced me only for an instant, his long nose aquiver. He could not brook insubordination, yet what was I to do but speak?

"How dare you interfere here?" he bellowed. "Get off with you!"

Nevertheless, I guessed I had moved him, and I would have staked anything that the craft was the *Mastico*. For the life of me, I had to go on.

"That paper —"

He was too young always to remember his rank: it came in fits and starts. His rage momentarily veered to curiosity, and some of his strict sense of the naval proprieties sloughed off.

"She flies the British ensign," the youth in him argued — but it conceded at the same time.

"Then, sir, she lies."

It may have been the strength of my words that recalled his position to him. Anyhow, my one moment of advantage passed, and he thundered:

"Get away! Get away, Rowntree, or I'll have you in the brig!"

No question of partiality now! I couldn't risk imprisonment with my enemy in sight. I knew he was remembering, puzzled, what he still considered my crazy first speech to him of stolen gold and paper; but my present words carried some amount of weight: I realized thus much as I anxiously watched one emotion chase another across the always self-betraying face of our commander.

Also, I soon noted that he was whispering to Lieutenant Porter, and that the Lieutenant nodded to the gun-crew grouped ready behind the long tube of iron at our prow. They sprang into action.

One man had already thrust the sponge down the gun's muzzle, twisted it, withdrawn it, knocked the dust free; another poured in the explosive, while a third and a fourth rammed home wad and shot. These movements I had seen without clearly classifying them, and the filling of the touch-hole with powder, and the sprinkling of certain grains along the breach; but now a stooped tar was squinting through the sight and, I was suddenly aware from Ray's teachings, getting its notch on a line somewhat below that spot in space which he wanted the ball to traverse.

Evidently, we were not going to be quite so inattentive as I had at first feared. At the sailor's elbow crouched a fellow who held, ready, a smouldering linstock.

Bainbridge shouted an order. Our man signalled the *Mastico* to come about. They got not the faintest response.

Bainbridge shouted again. We signalled that we'd fire if she didn't heed us.

Though she ducked her topsail by way of a signal in agreement, it was simply to gain a moment's time. The next, she was crowding all sail.

"By Heaven, I won't stand that!" cried our Captain. "Let her have it, boys!"

The man with the linstock instantly touched the priming. A flame issued from the gun — and a mighty roar. In less than a jiffy, our shot went straight across the *Mastico's* bows.

She lowered her red ensign as if in submission. Then, in laughing defiance, she ran up the pirate-flag of Tripoli!

The fat was in the fire at last.

"After her!" commanded Bainbridge, a-tingle with anger.

It seemed as if my wildest hopes were to be confirmed.

I could have cheered. The hunt begun at Cadiz was only interrupted, after all, at Algeciras.

As sure as Satan, Gonzales was on that ketch, and my pursuit of the stolen document might yet come to a successful issue. I was on tiptoes for the sight of the wretch.

Nor was my pursuit ever more intense. The ketch tacked. We tacked, too, but our larger size made us slower in comingabout, and we lost by the maneuvre. Then our greater power of canvas rushed us well toward her — and she tacked again.

It would probably have been mere waste of powder to continue firing at her. By as pretty seamanship as you could want to observe, except that we were too maddened to appreciate the thing as such, she would alter the range precisely as often as we found it.

"Belay that!" Bainbridge called to the gun-crew before they were ready for a second try. He salved his pride by adding to Porter, at his side:

"She's not worth it. We'll run her down and ram her — ram her!"

I hoped we might, but my heart was in my throat.

91

Since he said it, I felt sure I ought to believe him: he looked so fierce, so master of our frigate. Yet back and forth before that strip of coast immediately west of the city, the ketch doubled and doubled like a fleet hare before a racing hound. It was maddening.

Ten o'clock . . .

Eleven!

My eyes ached from staring at what was a picture for some famous marine-artist to paint: the unclouded sky, the salt breeze running up a light sea, we pounding along, and the *Mastico* impudently taunting us with her handicap of construction. Every time we drew near to her, I exulted — every time we were dodged, I jumped with chagrin. Well, there were others who must have been similarly affected, and more perilously because they controlled our destinies!

"This can't go on forever," said somebody in exasperation.

Our young Captain — oh, it may be that he was too young! — dropped his finally useless spy-glass and clenched his fists:

"I won't be mocked by her! It's gone on a bit too

92

long!"

"She could just as well" — that was Lieutenant Porter speaking, in oddly measured tones — "have made straight for the protection of the port. Why didn't she go there, sir?"

"Because she wants to make a fool of us," Bainbridge snapped in a rage. "Because she calls us 'the little, new nation over the seas' and thinks she can cajole more presents and more jewels out of us for her Sultan. Don't you understand we've got to head her off from there? — Put your helm down, helmsman — down!"

There were, later, those who said he had not soon enough thought of this policy; but then, people who've no business to, always tell you what you ought to have done while they stay safe from the consequences. At all events, he executed it too late: seven bells — and the ketch tacked under our very prow and headed into harbor.

CHAPTER VII

TO SLAVERY

A CRESENT-SHAPED harbor, with dim, mysterious African mountains on the Tunisian side, joined to the Atlasses near Kairwan: we ourselves were broadside to the mouth of the bay, which was said to be safe for ships drawing eighteen feet, though none too spacious. Buildings and vessels took on individuality, and a long line of rickety fortifications, virtually rimming the water's edge, came into view. I counted six lofty, Turkish-fashioned minarets tipping as many mosques.

"Come about!"

Bainbridge tossed his mane. I saw Porter's jaws tighten more and more, but he could not suppress his wonder:

"Are you going in, sir?"

The Captain spun around on him. "Is a United States frigate going to turn back?"

That naturally ended discussion and question — at least for the nonce. The lieutenant scarcely shrugged. With grim determination to punish her, we headed once more after the *Mastico*.

Tripoli rose in pleasant enough terraces from the sea, an interminable crenellated, somewhat pentagonal, wall with six bastions, mapping it out on its neck of low-lying land. The sands of the desert nearly touched its western fringe; eastward lay the green Meshiga Oasis where, over the Caramanlian sultanas' tombs, bulked the twelve-domed *kubba* of Hamonda; Porter, who had some acquaintance with the town, though little of the approach by sea, was naming these and other features to his superior:

"That's the Turkish quarter — there where the cupolas and minarets break the monotony of the pure Moorish houses. There's the Grand Mosque — and there's the Pasha Mosque — it used to be a Spanish church, they say."

The stone houses, comparatively few in number, belonged, it appeared, to the foreign consuls and the higher ranks of natives, and, in the case of the former only,

95

risked having windows on the streets. The prevailing, poorer population had their houses of one story only, built of earth and small stones and mortar, and forming a long line of flat roofs along which the swarming inhabitants could take long promenades. There was a superb marble arch, and even from afar, you got the effect of the noisy, colorful bazars.

Porter spoke as calmly as a hardened pleasure-traveller who wants to exhibit his knowledge before some voyaging friend new to the foreign panorama, but I noticed that his cool gaze did not long leave the flying *Mastico*. He was trying, I suppose, to conceal his disagreement with a commander for whom he entertained genuine affection — and who was at present listening to all he said with only a half-attentive ear.

Whatever Bainbridge comprehended of the cause, he cut short its effect, busying himself entirely with his ship, and only glancing ashore — and that, I took it, more to gauge military potentialities than anything else. Having decided what to do, he did it with his whole brain and heart.

Don't ask me about the merits of the case; they were

long later discussed at interminable length before a Naval Court of Inquiry. All I know is that the ordinary impulses of human nature pleaded for Bainbridge, who was, after all, exonerated: we had been mocked, and he resented it. A general low murmur around me made me sure that everyone on board resented it.

Now, moreover, while our intended victim drew us closer ashore nearly every time she tacked, Bainbridge did employ such precautions as were possible. Under his eager eyes he had Porter hold taut the chart provided by our Government, and he scanned its minute markings painstakingly. Besides, he ordered the lead heaved every two minutes.

"The approach as marked is simple — simple enough," he muttered. — Remember that through all this I hadn't fallen far away from him, merely keeping myself as small and quiet as possible to avoid his notice, so even his least speech came plain to my ears.

"Eight fathoms!" droned the man with the lead, not lifting his chin.

"A plenty," said Porter, who had at length visibly softened with acceptance of his chief's decision. "Only

— those shore-batteries, sir?"

"What do you know about them? Have you any information?"

"Nothing more than is hinted here, sir."

"That's not much."

"No, sir. But there's always Eaton's warning that we've a real enemy, and a wily one."

"Hum. Well, Eaton's not here to be more explicit — he's back home stirring up sentiment against these hordes, and I warrant he's right."

City and water-front lay oddly silent in the autumnal sun, as we drew ever diagonally nearer. Not a flag flew, or a sail, and the forts were dead things that gave never a sign of life. The ordinary movement of the city went on heedlessly as it were, almost too heedlessly. Porter remarked it — pronounced it queer — but Bainbridge remained dogged.

"Wait till the forts start," he decreed. "They must, finally. There's no large craft in there that can attack us. If the batteries get too hot, we can always retire, but I doubt if those half-dressed infidels know how to use them: they're famous for being bad shots."

98

Just then the *Mastico* cleverly tacked once more, and we were obliged to tack after her. Of course we lost time and space by the change, as we had all along been doing, and so we strained the harder, driving our prey directly landward, yet — through the tricks of that ketch's tacking — well to west of the harbor-centre. I don't believe it was a minute later that our lookout's warning broke over us:

"White water!"

Yes, it creamed about a mile straight ahead, water white and broken. Shoals — and not marked on the U. S. Navy's chart!

Doubt rode on the Lieutenant's face — on the Captain's, increased rage. Then, the *Mastico* was still maneuvering too rapidly for us to give her at last one of those shots we had so long withheld. One of the gunners, all ready to fire, spat disgustedly.

"Can we drop her before she gets there?" inquired Porter, meaning could we overhaul her before she, with her lighter draught, got nearer those rocks than would be safe for us.

He got no answer in words. We were tearing on at a

tremendous pace, a quarter-mile behind our flying
enemy. To be sure, wind and tide were with the pair
equally, but the frigate's size was a handicap — only
the ketch did appear to hesitate.

Bainbridge struck away the unreliable chart: a
random gust caught it and whirled it overboard. What
with hatred for its treason and chagrin at the taunting
tactics of the Moors, our commander was more than
ready to interpret favorably the seeming irresolution.

"He can't con her through! He can't do it! Lead,
there — *lead?*"

"Seven fathom, sir."

"As she goes, then," the Captain ordered that we
hold our course. "Steer small there — but as she goes!"

That hesitancy had decreased the ketch's vantage.
We plunged down toward her — her deck swarming
with hurrying men, a narrowing strip of blue between
us, and behind her the foaming water over what I later
learned was called Kaliusa Reef. Porter had, of course,
passed Bainbridge's command to our sailing-master;
fearlessly, at a full eight knots, we bounded forward,
our lower studding-sails raking the wave-tops. The

lead still gave us seven fathoms.

. Nearer — nearer! Now or never we would have the *Mastico.*

It was never.

The ketch luffed in the very nick of time. Exactly as we seemed to bestride her, she spun in a jiffy on her keel and bolted directly into the wind so close beside us that we could have jumped from our larboard rail right on to her.

A mortal trick. She was gone, and, while our men ran to brace yards, the *Philadelphia* struck, as that ketch had hoped she would — shivered — stood still. We were hard aground.

The concussion sent me sprawling to the deck. I bounced up almost instantly, but was no sooner afoot than I saw how dire was the damage done.

Owing to some cross-current of wind, no disturbance of the water had revealed this outer ledge; but the *Mastico's* master knew it and used it for his trap: he drew us on, dodged away — and our own chasing impetus impaled us. There were dark depths between us and the warning white-caps, but here we were tight

101

in, I should judge, less than twelve feet forward and a
scant seventeen abaft.

I don't pretend to take sides in the historic contro-
versy over what followed, but all my memory, as well as
all my sympathy, goes with our gallant Captain, whose
subsequent career proved his worth, and who then, at
most — befooled by our Government's imperfect charts
— had been led merely to rashness through the high
corridor of courage. It is always easy for inquiring-
boards and non-inquiring newspapers to shriek condemnation. As for me, I shall always see Captain Bainbridge, his hat knocked off or thrown away — his long
nose quivering — his hair blowing — as he sprang from
here to there and vociferated his commands:

"Lay all sails aback! . . . Loose the topgallants!
. . . It's blowing fresh: give us a heavy press of canvas,
and back her off!"

Every man-jack of us was with Bainbridge then.
We cast three anchors from the bows. When the report
came that water was started in the hold, we hove three-
quarters of our guns overboard. Back her off? I've
heard there are some who say it could still have been

done. I believe that, short of three solid days devoted to the job, we might as well have tried to tow the mainland out to sea.

"Save some ordinance!" pleaded square-jawed Porter. "They'll be after us now!"

They were — immediately, with us helplessly pinned on our rock. As if it had all been stage-arranged, that harbor, which a moment since was utter somnolence, jumped into hostile life.

"*Bang!*"

Eastward of us, one of the fortress-walls emitted a flash — a report: a roundshot whistled over my head. It was plain that they, too, were ready, exultantly waiting the sure signal of our impalement. The whole of that fort spurted fire and sound — and the next fort — and the next. We were in a rain of iron, while, ship by ship, the vessels in the harbor — mariners squirming up to their rigging — crowded sail and ran enemy-colors to the forepeaks.

"*Here they come!*"

They came indeed like an army of locusts, and as ruthless — at least twenty different types, from occidental ships, captured and converted, to felucca and xebec, crazy craft many of them, but vindictive and lusty for loot. Shots from our remaining guns proved as futile as pea-shooter-pops; the pirates were upon us like a veritable fleet, and at their forefront rode the baleful *Mastico* before we could have launched our small-boats to escape, had we the mind to — even before we had half served-out our side-arms.

Bainbridge issued the inevitable command:

"Prepare to receive boarders!"

They surrounded the frigate, closed upon her, bumped — larboard, starboard and astern. The crews of those behind, using the vessels in front as gangways, the screaming mass of them charged down and across our deck.

Brown and bearded and dirty, they pressed us from every side until we perforce formed a little group, back to back, at centre of amidships. They were all naked to the waist; they bore queer pistols, curved swords, flame-shaped knives, musketoons and terrifying carbines. We would give them our best, that was sure, but they were a host, we a handful.

104

"Scuttle ship!" our Captain bawled.

Led by Porter, some of our men fought a way through that mob and started to obey the order. They were too late, though: as it turned out later, foemen followed at their heels and repaired each piece of damage as soon as it was done.

Somehow, I stood with a chopping cutlass in hand at the outer edge of us Americans. How much real harm I inflicted is another question, but, anyway, nobody would then have complained of me as too immature and sensitive, and my face burned red with eagerness to do my part. Blades rang upon mine, frowning dark faces fronted me — open mouths which hissed alien curses, and spat — always spat. I could fence a bit, and I had to employ that talent, although I noticed that more knocks than cuts were offered — more blows than bullets. Anyhow, I was risen above fear to a sort of triumphant despair, when the rank just in front of me was thrust open and two figures crowded out.

One of these I recognized. My cutlass suicidally faltered.

Again his black eyes blazing, his countenance all

105

saturnine glee, facing me, was our erstwhile Vice Consul at Cadiz. His scimitar was poised above my undefended head, and he stood over me a-tiptoe, the thief of that State-letter I had so wanted to recover.

He was almost a fine figure of a man now, in his clothes of the best sea-cloth. He wore big silver buckles on his shoes, and the buttons on his waistcoat were new George guineas, which his pirate crew had doubtless rifled from some dead or captive Englishman, since I last saw him in Algeciras harbor. I was no longer any use to him living. Smaller than me, he yet, because of my lowered blade, had me at his mercy — and mercy was the last thing he intended to show.

"You die, you pup of a meddler!" — He yelled it through his yellow teeth.

I tried to raise my weapon, but I had no doubt at the moment that his prophesy would be fulfilled. Then the second figure, while it beat my steel away, seized at Ventura's wrist.

"By Allah," that person cried — and, strangely enough, in Spanish, "do you not know that the Pasha wants not dead men, but slaves? How can the General-

106

issimo get jewels for his fingers in return for flesh that is cold?"

Nevertheless, the threatened blow fell, yet with far less force than expected. The blade must have been so deflected that I got only the flat of it on my crown.

Of a sudden, I had a first glimpse of the interferer. It was — it couldn't be, yet it was that rogue of a Spanish gypsy, Silverio!

The next instant — crash! Consciousness ran out of me as if lightning ran out of my eyes . . .

Well, I have small cause to be grateful to the fellow whom I call Gonzales, but for that whack I thank him: it hid from my vision the humiliation that followed. The next thing I clearly knew, I was one of a band of prisoners being hustled out of a long-boat on to firm ground — and, behind us, the American flag had been lowered on the U.S. Frigate *Philadelphia*.

CHAPTER VIII

YUSUF, PASHA

THE sun of that October 31st set upon a scene disasterous for the young American Navy — and upon private and special desolation for its newest volunteer. Our frigate *Philadelphia* was become a prize of the Tripolitan pirates at the very harbor-mouth before their capital, her entire personnel were at their mercy — if they had any — and as for me, I had overtaken our recreant Cadiz Vice Consul, Gonzales, only to fall a prisoner in the hands of these barbarous folk whom he appeared now to be serving.

Our officers were landed. I was half dragged ashore, the cool water bringing me full consciousness; but, the surf running so high as to make beaching the boats a trouble, our men were thrown out, rods from land, and forced to fight their way to terra firma. Then the hands of each of us were lashed behind him with stout half-inch rope, and a count of the noses was taken, which our captured papers made possible.

Not one was missing. So greedy had been those raiders that our clothes, even, were largely stripped from off us — even to Bill Ray's silver finger-rings, though they did, by some oversight, leave the brass circlets in his ears. Nevertheless, despite the attack's ferocity and the infliction of many a distressing wound, the buccaneers had respected their pasha's desire for slaves and his eye toward possible ransoms: incredible as it might seem they had taken no toll in human life. Three hundred and seven, including me as stowaway, we sailed from Gibraltar — three hundred and seven we totalled still.

It was night at last, I should say about ten o'clock, when the crew were marched off in one direction and the officers in another. On Bainbridge's plea that I was a mere lad and had been badly banged about, I — still dizzy from a terrific headache, though really nothing more — was grudgingly placed in his care.

I saw big Wilson hulk off, the one shoulder sullenly higher than the other; and, in the light of a Tripolitan's flaming torch, Bill Ray waved me goodbye. That astonishing man, clad in not much more than his shirt,

109

was, or pretended to be, as cheerful as a cherub:

"Avast there," he called to me, "remember my advice, hearty; do what they tell you to, and do it neat as pie. That's the secret of a happy life for a mariner!"

I hated to be thus separated from him, knowing not what punishment or disaster might befall him, though knowing full well he would accept it without outward sign of suffering; for through long hours of association I had come to love this big, uncouth sailorman. There was no choice, however, and I could not even summon a smile of assurance to give him.

Heavily guarded, our party began to ascend streets narrow, tortuous, filthy, along which jeering folk in strange clothes, even women from behind their veils, flung curses at us. The men spat, the spittle making a continuous clicking sound on the cobble-stones.

Our shame could not have weighed us down more had we known — what was a fact — that, at this very juncture, a prize-crew had cleared the *Philadelphia*, favored by a wind-shift and strong boats to tow her from Kaliusa Reef, bringing her close in to shore. Like the meanest criminals, we were driven into the court-yard of a sort of castle, being an irregular, square pile of masonry imposing enough; and so through a winding and darkened passage until I stood with my companions blinking, after the outer darkness, in the very centre of a vast and extravagantly illuminated room.

The light was supplied by scores of curiously wrought lamps suspended from a lofty ceiling and covered with glass of various colors; they revealed that the apartment was ornately built of marble, and that along its walls were grouped more and more sinister-looking soldiers who bore a forest of semi-oriental muskets, pikes and halberds. There wasn't a stick of furniture in the huge hall, except at the farther end, where, surrounded by men whose rich robes and jewels showed them to be high functionaries, was erected a canopied divan, and on that sat, crosslegged, about the fattest person you can imagine.

Cushions of cloth-of-gold bolstered him up. He wore a garment that I thought at first a yellow dressing-gown — my grandfather had a dressing-gown very like it — there was an enormous gem-studded turban poised on his head, and he gleamed, in fact, all over with jewels;

111

but he wasn't a pleasant picture. Most fat men are
jolly; this one's sallow cheeks were so loose and heavy
that they pulled down the corners of his lax mouth
above its straggling beard. His nose was hooked, and,
over a pair of bags of black skin, two narrow, calculating
eyes shone at us, more of a snake's than you are likely to
view in any human countenance as long as you live in
Christian countries.

"This must be America's arch-enemy," whispered
Bainbridge to me, for I was just beside him — "Yusuf,
the Pasha of Tripoli — the Pasha who dispossessed his
brother Hamet."

I looked about in vain for Gonzales — for Silverio —
and vainly wondered just what their connection could
be with this odd, but luxurious, court. All the barba-
rians' faces, however, were unknown to me so far as I
could make out, and nobody else broke the profound
silence until the potentate himself muttered something
that sounded like:

"Sidi Mahommed Dghies?"

Out of the crowd a man stepped and bobbed his head
to a low obeisance. He was a stoutish personage himself

and plainly fond of the flesh-pots, only his tonnage was nothing to compare with his sovereign's.

"Son of the Prophet," said he in a silky voice, "Conqueror and Great!"

He used, of course, the native tongue to utter this, the ruler's ceremonial title, but I learned that much, and a bit more, of their lingo before I grew many days older: when you hear the same phrases over and over, obsequiously pronounced, whenever the ruler of the land is addressed, you can't help guessing that it's nothing but a phrase of enforced flattery. As he spoke, we saw Sidi in profile; he had a snub nose and a merry eye, the only thing, in fact, in the entire glum assemblage to suggest happiness; yet I thought that even here there lurked something hard and untrustworthy.

Bainbridge said to me, very softly, glad, I knew, to count me his friend:

"Sidi Mahommed. He is the *kaya*, I remember. Eaton spoke of him. None too well, I think. The *kaya's* the lord chief justice, or Grand Judge of the entire shindy — when the fat man yonder doesn't scowl at the judgments he gives."

113

The Pasha barely inclined his turbaned head in response to Sidi's greeting. He turned from him and demanded, exactly as if he were the schoolmaster taking the count of his class:

"The aga? Ibrahim Bey?"

And, if you please, out stepped a figure only too recognizable to me — to my sorrow. So it was he who commanded the Turkish troops in this tyrannical Tripoli, which showed no respect for the laws of any country other than Turkey, and little enough there, where it was nominally subject. He bowed in turn, but he bowed nearly to the floor; until now hidden behind his betters, Mr. Wigglesworth's Vice Consul again.

Ibrahim Bey? So Ventura Gonzales' real name was Turkish!

Immediately, I realized why he had to be addressed in Spanish aboard the *Philadelphia*. He was a Turk, ignorant of the Arabic speech of Tripoli, representing the "Porte," but doubtless selling his services as spy to Yusuf Pasha. And the letter? This was surely his first landing since Algeciras. He had had no good chance to negotiate it as yet.

114

Through Sidi as interpreter, the fat tyrant bade Ventura — I mean Ibrahim — tell his story, and, without even a glance in our direction, he told it. He began with a quick sketch of American naval conditions as he had gathered them to be during his residence in Cadiz. I think they were pretty accurate — certainly none too complimentary to our sixteen States; but next, he got right on to our loss of the *Philadelphia*, and then he threw truth overboard.

I looked again for Silverio — no sign of him. He was not at the court tonight.

Meanwhile, humble, almost cringing in his bearing, Gonzales yet managed this part of his narrative so that you would have thought he had tricked us completely by his own personal skill, as his own sailing-master of the *Mastico*, and had then boarded us and captured us single-handed. As his yellow fangs nursed each succeeding exaggeration, I saw Sidi smile superciliously, the merriment in his eyes ever increasing; and I could feel Bainbridge struggle to keep down in his heart a denial which, if declared, might prove dangerous interruption to such formal proceedings. That mountain of royal flesh, cross-legged on the divan, remained impassive, and the rows of armed soldiers never moved a muscle.

So much I noted, and one thing more: the Turk said nothing of his theft. I did not belong in this story, nor yet did that final night at the Consulate. This omission should perhaps have been attributed to the extremely important and delicate nature of the document stolen. Ibrahim was, maybe, saving it for a private interview. Nevertheless, I had the conviction that he was saving it to sell, when opportunity offered, to one of those greater powers almost equally interested in its contents and likely to pay a handsomer price than the fat, and plainly avaricious, Yusuf; I had also the conviction that Gonzales felt he had plenty of time to play one possible customer against another and thus make the best bargain for himself.

Anyhow, he ended his brag at last. The Pasha said something which Sidi interpreted as a regal willingness to hear whatever Bainbridge had to say:

"Out of his goodness, bright as the sun at noon and complacent as the sun at setting, the Conqueror of the

Great expresses a willingness to hear any explanation or excuses that the American Captain would like to offer him."

Bainbridge took a couple of steps forward.

His severest critics would have had to admire him then. Although he had not been quite half stripped of his clothes, his uniform was badly torn — I remember how the gilt braid dangled sadly from one of his coat's big lapels — and the riot of his hair was wild. He had a bruise already black under his right side-whisker and a slight cut on the opposite cheek. He was a captive — a commander who had lost his ship at least in part because of his hot-headedness. And yet he was a figure to respect.

He bowed just enough and no more. When he spoke, it was in the shortest and most dignified way. He didn't deign to present any arguments at all in confutation of Ibrahim Bey's self-vaunting lies: he simply made a brief statement of what had taken place, and requested for his officers and crew the treatment proper to prisoners-of-war.

There was something so splendidly just in his manner

117

that honestly I don't know but he would have got it if
nothing had tampered with the situation at that moment. Once, the over-nourished and over-flattered
sovereign up there on the divan, despite his known pre-
deliction for enslaving all captured Christians, actually
nodded. What changed everything was the entrance
into the room of a tall, blond European, who shouldered
his way forward as Bainbridge ceased speaking and who,
I soon learned, was the energetic and well-intentioned
Consul of Denmark at Tripoli, Nicholas Nissen.

Mussulmen do not like interruptions, and this was
even a royal court of Mussulmen. At once the gaze of
the fat Pasha resumed its likeness to that of a watchful
serpent.

"To what," he asked — through Sidi Mahommed —
"do we owe this unrequested visit when we are in the
midst of considering important matters of State?"

Nicholas Nissen was a conscientious and courageous
representative of his country. Later, the captives were
deeply indebted to him, but now his impulsiveness did
us no good. It might have been better had he shown
some timidity, but that was not his way, and he would

never be discommoded. Instead, he replied:

"My intrusion is due to a knowledge of Your Majesty's far-famed benevolence. May it continue a hundred years."

"Hum," grunted Yusuf, when this was translated. The scowls on his loosely hung face were grown suspicious. "Speak on."

Mr. Nissen was come here on an errand of mercy, as he conceived it. He had been told of the rough treatment of the prisoners, and his sense of humanity had been touched. He resumed:

"Having heard through all the city of Your Majesty's recent triumph, I thought it my duty to request some leniency for that triumph's victims. I come here, having no doubt —"

But he never got any further, nor was I ever able to understand how this best-willed of men did not know better the master with whom he was now dealing and had dealt for so long. The Pasha of Tripoli might listen with pleased attention to the arguments of a fallen foe; but he was the last monarch in the world to brook suggestions from an alleged disinterested party: those bags

119

under his small eyes grew blacker, and his abnormally broad face went pure purple. He looked as if he was going into a fit; he altered permanently for the worse the whole atmosphere of our plight as, well nigh sitting erect, he fair roared: -

"These victims" — that was the way that the ever-smiling *kaya*, Sidi, finally rendered it — "are no concern of Denmark! They are the captives of our victorious arms, through Allah's favor — *Allah Allah Mohammed ben Allah* — and as such they shall be held for ransom like any and all other of our captured foes! Are our soldiers to protect our shores with no rewards for their bravery?"

Nissen tried to explain that all he meant was fair play —

"Fair play?" The tyrant nearly got to his slippered feet. "Did I not have to haul down his rag from its staff in May because the Prince of America did not wish to pay any more to let his merchant-ships sail up and down my Mediterranean? The smooth-faced unbeliever sometimes grows wily, but he need not think he can be less generous with me than with my neighbors.

120

He found time to build a beautiful frigate for the Dey of Algiers, and Tunis has always all she wants. Why; is it not current that presents are given to all? Not long ago, the Admiral wanted a gold-headed cane, a gold watch and twelve pieces of cloth. The Prime Minister wanted a double-barrelled gun and a chain of gold. The Aga of the 'Porte' said he'd like some jewelry, and the other officials naturally asked for sugar and coffee and tea. Well, didn't they get all they wanted? Why shouldn't we?"

I saw by the quivering of Bainbridge's long nose that his temper had snapped at last. He tossed his head.

"Sir —" he started.

"You mean 'Your Majesty,'" Ventura grinned, and his yellow fangs shone evilly.

"I call no king that," cried our Captain, "who fails to abide by the laws of civilized warfare. Ransom! What happened to me in 1800, when I commanded the 'Washington'? In order to please the Dey of Algiers and finally follow the orders of Consul O'Brien, I was obliged to take the Algerian Consul to Constantinople instead of sailing for home. Not only that; I had to hoist the Algerian flag at the main, and carry passengers amounting to two hundred persons in the suite of the Ambassador, with their luggage and horses and sheep and the lions and tigers and antelopes that they intended to offer to the Sultan. Never again will I yield to the childish freak of a royalty that has no right to exist. Tell your Pasha, Mr. Mahommed, that I — and my country — have done with payments to him forever. The United States of America will not pay a penny of ransom as long as she has one gun left to her name, and the *Philadelphia*, he may be assured, is not our only frigate!"

It was a deadly declaration, though I misdoubt much could have been gained, in the Pasha's now stormy temper, by a fairer. Sidi Mahommed tried to get Bainbridge to soften it before interpretation, but Bainbridge was himself too angry: he had not yet learned the perils of surrendering to rages for however just a cause. Moreover, his excited expression of physiognomy, and his clenched fists could not be explained by soft words to the reptile-eyed potentate.

From purple to livid went the Pasha. For almost a

minute he could hardly speak. When he could and did, his sentence of us was thus rendered, silkily, through his Grand Judge:

"Unbelievers belonging to the Prince of the United States of America, the civilization of the Prophet is the civilization of the faithful. What is your puny nation that it should expect more of us than any other enemy of God? You are but prisoners, and you have dared to come even to our Bay of Tripoli without bringing tribute, without any present of anything, even the slightest jewel like a pretty diamond ring for our sovereign. You are Christian dogs whom Heaven has surrendered to our prowess. No ransom? No tribute? Very good. Allah has made you slaves, and slaves you shall remain."

CHAPTER IX

RENEGADES

R IGHT upon his petulant decision, the pirate-monarch rose with gouty laboriousness. He waved his jeweled hands helplessly for aid. Sidi Mahommed was close to him and offered his shoulder on the one side; Ibrahim Bey anticipated a pair of native servants and nimbly leaped to assist on the other. The court remained immobile during the royal exit.

Then, with no further show of deference, an officer of the guard gave a lively command, the soldiers clinked their weapons, rushed forward and surrounded the Americans who had been herded here. Prodded by the butts of muskets, often by the boots of our conductors, we were hustled out of the luxurious apartment, back through the dim courtyard with its sound of happy fountains and its odors of hidden flowers, and, by roundabout dirty streets, to the quarters that were to

124

be ours. Such of the wondering populace as was still abroad jeered or threw rotten oranges and mandarins at us, laughing uproariously when one hit its mark and splashed, broken, against a burning cheek.

.The crew were housed in one prison, the officers (and I with them) in another; but, through the under-current of convict-communication that somehow occurs among respectable prisons as well as among those of disrepute, we soon learned that there was little to choose between our two residences for comfort. Mere rags were doled out to all alike for clothing, and what any of us had of the slightest value or desirability was ripped from us; the food, saving for a liberality of native fruits, was scant and vile and irregular. Olives, figs and dates were our salvation, the dates being very fine. There were often plenty of oranges and lemons, the sweeter lemons that we rarely see at home. It was a kind of barley gruel that was doled out to us mostly, and that was generally both badly cooked and rancid.

A slatternly soldier delivered one of us from a degree of suffering and ignominy. He appeared the second evening, while we were trying to choke down, for hunger's sake, some of that soured barley, and primitively having to use our fingers for forks.

"Doctor," he demanded. "Which man here honorable Señor doctor?" He spoke in halting Spanish, our only intelligible ground for communication.

Dr. Cowdery rose, rather a sorry looking figure in the rags he had been granted, but plainly master of his profession.

"I am the doctor," said he. "What do you want with me?"

"Son of Prophet sick. Face turn all black. Son of Prophet want eat big banquet-dinner tonight with much music and dance. Doctor here no good, Son of Prophet had cut off arms. Doctor of Prince of America come cure."

Fortunately, Cowdery, from a mere look at the Pasha ensconced on his divan that first night, had diagnosed his case — a malady of the veins — and, from his knowledge of science, was able to allay the "Conqueror of the Great's" sufferings without rendering the fat man too wrathful. This meant that our doctor soon spent a good quarter of his time at the palace. He always went there between guards, but, when he pleased the Sovereign, it gave him chance to wheedle favors for the rest of us.

Some amelioration reached us, too, through the renewed pleas of unabashed Mr. Nissen, who bounced back from rebuff like a rubber ball. It appeared that, not so long ago, our Consul Eaton had rendered inestimable service to Denmark by buying on credit several Danish prizes in Tunis, and Mr. Nissen was bound and determined to show his appreciation to America as represented by her prisoners in Tripoli: there was no keeping him down, and he accepted the Pasha's fits of irascibility and injustice as momentary inconveniences, whereas he always profited by the merest hint of good temper. Moreover, Lieutenant Porter organized a school for naval instruction, in our scant leisure, among his juniors, whereat I — the last of my fanciful humors slain by cruel realities — little by little qualified for the Service, should luck ever come to serve.

Yet nothing effectually altered our sad lot. We were beyond mercy today and apparently beyond hope for tomorrow. Ransom in the terms of thousands of dollars was our only hope of release. In May, 1801, the Pasha had taken it into his head to increase the annual levy of $83,000, and the "Prince of America" was at last aroused, after much dallying, not only on Mr. Jefferson's part but on the entire nation's, to fight for our rights. The Barbary States had become regular blackmailers. Nevertheless, it was doubtful if we should not have accepted the insults to our flag and continued to "treat" with the Easternmost of these piratical countries had not our Mediterranean merchants clamored louder for armed protection than our pinch-pennies and politicians at home grumbled at taxes.

I thought more of Ibrahim Bey than of politics. Always there was the thought of his treachery and his ultimate success with his theft. Almost anything might happen because of my having fallen asleep over Mr. Wigglesworth's dull tomes. Bainbridge alone lifted me above my preoccupations.

He had lost his ship in circumstances that might be construed to ruin an otherwise unspotted record. He had led himself and his men to this captivity. Yet he held his head high, and if his martinet manner softened to those under him, and his former impetuosity temporarily disappeared, he kept his dignity and won affection. As I hope never to see a man more sorely tried, so I know that I can never see disaster more nobly borne.

With it all, his mind was never quiescent. One saw him constantly fretting, and the weight of responsibility for the sufferings of his men was heavy on his young shoulders. At length, choosing a day when Cowdery assured him that Yusuf was in high good humor, not having too much indulged lately in his favorite foods, Captain Bainbridge had his desire translated to one of our captors, a brigand of a fellow, who had taken pleasure in being particularly objectionable.

"I have a request to put before the Pasha," said he, "and, in order to put it, I should appreciate an audience with him."

Before the guard could refuse with a native oath, our commander produced a shiny gold piece, from I know not what place of hiding, so thoroughly had we been despoiled of all articles of value. The native first opened wide his lazy, dark eyes, then bowed with his head nearly touching the ground.

"Anything that the Señor Captain wishes," he prom-

129

ised, and left the squalid room of our imprisonment backwards rapidly.

"Gold is a powerful language," said Bainbridge with a grim smile.

"Will you get the audience, sir?" said I, marvelling.

"What with Yusuf's health and this scoundrel's happiness, I have no doubt of it," he declared; but then, at once, he ignored me and the others and began pacing the floor in profound thought.

Half an hour later, so magical was that disk of gold, he was smilingly summoned to follow the guard. A nod in my direction brought me, too. At the hint of demur in the native's face, Bainbridge explained:

"It is etiquette that the Captain should have an escort; it is also courtesy to your Pasha."

Thus it was that I again saw Yusuf. We were conducted through the same dirty streets and the same courtyard, a beautiful octagon by day, with all the windows of the palace peeping down upon it. The pasha was bolstered up among his inevitable cushions, under a sort of canopy, while two very black negroes fanned him with ostrich plumes.

The Pasha wore a complacent smile and did not at all notice us at first. He was intently watching some scantily clad children, the largest of whom had just extracted a deadly looking scorpion with eight wicked eyes from under a stone, and was holding it tightly by the last joint of the tail. The child pushed it nearly into the faces of his comrades — all little Yusufs probably — and made them scream as they tried to escape, while the Pasha clapped his hands delightedly. Then, with a cruel twist accompanied by an impudent grin, the young torturer broke off the tip of the creature's sting and let the scorpion loose.

Bainbridge gave me a significant glance. Then, preceded by the ever bowing and smiling attendant, we approached the fat ruler of Tripoli.

He was all affability.

"The Captain of the frigate in the harbor has come to offer us a present?" was finally translated.

Bainbridge replied with the utmost respect, letting the suggestion pass over his head:

"Conqueror of the Great," said he, acquiesing, for policy's sake, in use of the title, "I am come to request

131

leave to write my report, giving my version of the facts, to my superior, Commodore Preble, and to ask that this be conveyed to the *Vixen* under flag-of-truce."

Yusuf rubbed his hands and swayed a little where he sat. Out of the corners of his heavily-pouched eyes he continued to watch the children approvingly.

"Supply the American Captain with quills and paper," he ordered, waving his fat hand. "He will write his report in his quarters, and you shall bring it to me, and I will please him by sending it to the officer he speaks of under flag-of-truce." The Pasha looked away from both children and us now; his meditative gaze rested on the disabled scorpion, dragging itself and its paralyzed tail, back to the shelter of a stone, where it might slowly die. "I am glad," said Yusuf softly, "that my prisoners are beginning to see reason. Take the American Captain and his companion-prisoner away, and tell him that he is to insert in his report a demand for $50,000 ransom."

Bainbridge drew himself up to his top height as this was translated:

"As I told the Pasha," said he, his indignation barely

controlled, I knew, "there is no more question of tribute and ransom. I cannot ask for this in my report; I can simply state the facts as they occurred, and trust to the sense of equity of Tripoli's ruler to have a truthful account of what happened presented to my superior."

All the venom in Yusuf's nature returned. He waved his arms. He shrieked his disapproval of us, and, I have no doubt, of all our countrymen and all our personal ancestors. There was no further time for translations. Servants appeared from behind walls of mosaic and shoved us ruthlessly from the irate royal presence.

No report would be delivered to Preble unless it were written practically at the dictation of Yusuf; Bainbridge would not write a report, however much his honor depended on the truth reaching the outside world, unless he could write it as a simple statement of facts. There was an impasse, and we re-began, without hope of amelioration, our incarceration.

CHAPTER X

BASTINADOED

TO MAKE an end of this catalogue of woes, although our officers did not have to work, like myself and some of the men, by night, our labor at any hour proved gruelling. The amount exacted was nigh superhuman. We were systematically insulted because of our faith and our nationality (nobody in this wretched land seeming to know that the United States of America was more than some rich tyranny beyond the seas); a few of the wounded died.

For the rest, the lash hung ever over our backs, and beside our drivers stood armed men whose orders were to pay insubordination with death, or so we were told. I doubt if this order would have been carried out, for the avaricious Yusuf folded his plump hands and waited confidently for the "Prince of America," as he persisted in calling him, to offer an armed frigate or some other trifle in return for the *Philadelphia's* prisoners.

Meanwhile, we were set to repairing one of the age-weakened bastions of the city, hewing and carrying stones. It was in the very shadow of one of those forts with battlemented walls which look across the crescent-shaped harbor toward the old Sixteenth-Century citadel — a strip of land favored as a promenade for native gentry. These gentry would stand and stare at us with a sort of proprietary interest.

They surveyed us as if we were cows or pigs at a county fair, but, after all, they finally passed on. It was those slave-drivers with their whips who made life well nigh unbearable. Because Bill Ray was big and husky-looking, and did his work neat as pie with never a grumble, they imposed on him until he was near to dead from overwork and undernourishment. With an aching heart I watched his shoulders slump every day a little more — a little more.

Not only that, but Gus Wilson, his old enemy, big though he was, seemed inexplicably favored in the tasks assigned him. Never did a curling lash fall on his back, never, save at the very first, were those abominable Arab curses, accompanied by vicious kicks, aimed at

135

him. In fact, he was almost ignored, and so were a
number of his cronies. I wondered why.

Bill and I and several other prisoners were set, one
intolerably hot day — for Tripoli, unlike Tunis, has a
climate of extreme ups and downs — to transferring a
certain heap of huge stones to the walls and setting them
in place. It was evident that Bill's strength was exhausted.

"Well," he grinned at me with pathetic cheerfulness,
"here's where you'll see the end of a happy mariner."

I looked sharply around. Our little gang of workmen
was, for the moment, alone, and behind the pile of
stones a man could stay concealed for a goodly space of
time in the deep shadows.

"Sit there," said I, "and get back your strength.
I'll warn you the minute those devils come our way, but
it'll give you breathing-time."

He was all for demurring, but with no great effort I
pushed him down.

"I'm not tired," I insisted, "and we eat better in our
barracks than you do in yours."

He lay there panting in a state of semi-collapse, and

we others put our shoulders to our tasks while he gradually regained a modicum of vitality and something of his old courage. Nevertheless we, who were a weary three, could not accomplish the work of four. After a full half-hour, our task-masters, busied in a violent personal discussion, remembered about us and came in our direction on the run. I hastily hauled Bill to his feet.

Just at that moment, Gus Wilson happened to look round. He saw my act and gave a nasty leer toward us. He had hated me ever since that day when I first circumvented him on the *Philadelphia*. Also, he had no love for Bill.

Now he hunched up his deformed shoulder and nodded significantly at one of our overseers, who turned his attention to the stone heap. But the tail-end of that nod had included Bill ominously.

"Someone has been shirking," the whip-brandisher yelled, regarding the stone-pile malevolently. "Someone — or all."

He said this in his native tongue, but there was no misunderstanding him. He was for attacking us all, but

137

that might have required undue exertion on his part, and four were a big proposition. It was suddenly made clear that, though someone must be punished, one might take the place of all.

There is a fiendish love of cruelty in these native Tripolitans. This fellow approached Bill, whose big, kindly face was still white from weariness. The other two men of the workers were nearly equally worn out. There could be no doubt about it: my youth was in my favor, and I was in no bad condition physically in spite of all our hardships, having the resiliency of my young years.

As the lash was about to descend I pushed forward. Bill tried to hold me back, but, for once, I was the stronger.

"It was my fault," I whispered to my friend. "I can never hold up my head again if they touch you. Say nothing, or I can't forgive you."

As a matter of fact, he had no chance, for my whispering condemned me as guilty. Bill was hustled back with the other two to that stone-lifting, now under frowning surveillance.

138

The overseer was in a fury. Because his back had been turned, because he had probably lost in his petty discussion with his mate, he had to vent his bloodthirstiness on somebody at once, especially as that mate was now shrugging derisively.

The day neared dark. I was tossed to the ground and held fast.

But it was not with his whip that the man attacked me: it was with a pliable lath of bamboo — tap, tap, tap, ever so lightly on the soles of my feet. I knew the process only by repute, but it had been whispered ominously among us prisoners that a skilful bastinadoist can, actually, by the easy, but regular, continuation of his blows, kill a victim after a sufficient number of hours of punishment. I tried to rivet my mind on other things.

Tap — tap — tap —

How long did this torturer mean to keep it up?

I knew I had an attentive crowd of natives within view of me, watching indolently. Perhaps half an hour passed, three-quarters, when who should come by, taking the late afternoon air, but the Kaya and Lord

Chief Justice Sidi Mahommed Dghies!

Half amused, he paused. I made out that he inquired of the guards concerning my case. The expert occupied with me stayed his strokes to reply. After he had ended, huge Wilson, with a shrug of his deformed shoulder, supplemented in Spanish, in his thin, little voice:

"Besides which, my Excellency, the boy has told a lie."

Here was the long-waited-for chance for Gus to vent his venom. It must have pleased him more to use it today against me than against Bill Ray: I had always managed to slip like an eel out of his power; once that he got hold of the eel, he would hold it in a tight squeeze. This was surely why the giant had denounced me to the supervisors; it might explain this further denunciation. Yet I could not make out how Wilson, a slave like the rest of us, dared to address so lofty an official as the Kaya.

Sidi only stroked his beard. Softly he made inquiry. "A lie about what?"

This put Gus in a pretty quandary. With nearly all

140

the other prisoners around, within earshot, to contradict any false answer, he was obliged shamefacedly to admit that I had merely assumed another's guilt, and I felt a general stir of sympathy about me.

"Why, if what you say be so," declared Sidi, with a twinkle in his dark eyes as he regarded Gus, "the lad deserves reward, not punishment."

Wilson stared, sullenly, fearfully, but he durst not reply.

Sidi went on:

"You told me yesterday that you were faithfully studying the holy book — the Koran. Do you not yet know that the Koran bids us heal stripes suffered for any friend?"

In the midst of my pain, all the worse it seemed now the taps were temporarily stopped, I wondered why Gus, of all men in the world, should engage in a course of reading, and how such an uncouth person could continue without impunity this almost private speech with the dignitary there. But the dignitary chuckled in a sort of cynic kindliness.

"Weren't you," he asked me where I still lay, "cabin

141

boy to the American Captain whom our invincible forces conquered?"

I nodded.

"That pleases me," said he, rubbing his hands. "You will, to be sure, continue this work for Tripoli's continued prowess the rest of the time, but twice daily you shall serve me — at noon and evening. The creature who has been doing that service spilled a dish of my favorite *kababs* a few hours since." The Kaya gave a heavy sigh: "I was compelled to have his hands cut off. The presence of a Christian waiter will be diverting in my household. Can you walk?"

At a gesture from my new master, I was hauled to an upright position by two natives. Sidi Mahommed's words sounded to me as doubtful favor; Wilson's blue eyes lowered. I stood stiffly. Gingerly I tried to take a step or two, tottering at first from the pain and making a wry face. Nevertheless, there might be advantage for us all in my new position!

"I can do it," I said, stubbornly beating down the smarting stings of my heels.

"Then," ordered Sidi, again waving his far arm and

142

waddling ahead, "come with me."

He moved off, with never a further look to right or left. Somehow or other, Bill and the other two stone-heavers who had earlier worked with me were in the group close by. More from pain than anything else, I hesitated, but as I did so, I caught Bill's comforting whisper almost in my ear:

"Go along, my hearty. Do what you have to do and do it neat as pie. That's the rule as makes a happy life for a mariner — even ashore."

I could not answer, but I gave him as much of a grin as I could summon for reply: it seemed the very persistence of good advice. Sidi walked slowly — for his own ease, not mine — and I hobbled a respectful half-yard behind him. Fortunately the bastinadoing had been of comparatively short duration: I already felt I should soon overcome the worst of its effects.

Meanwhile, from certain chuckling sounds ahead, and an occasional shaking of his plump back, Sidi appeared in high good-humor. Indeed, he really must have been exceedingly pleased with himself, partly because of his new acquisition and partly, I gathered,

143

because he had disgruntled Wilson; the Kaya belonged to that class of outwardly merry and careless good livers who, nevertheless, like to assert annoying power over the self-same underlings upon whom they rely for important work. Sidi had a happy way with him of raising hopes — and then dashing them to earth.

Presently, as we passed the old Roman triumphal arch that stands a bit off from the port, he turned his head and smiled back at me:

"That sulky giant said you lied. Anyone can see you have the wrong kind of eyes: you are not skilful enough to practice the art of lying. He envies you your luck. Ha!"

I did not know if the etiquette of my new position permitted reply; but, if I were not skilful enough to lie, I was unruly enough to have a retort ready: "Gus," said I, "is nothing but a bully."

The Kaya gave me a flash of interest: "Then you do not think he will make a good follower of the great Prophet?"

"A Mohammedan, sir?" This was an astounding suggestion.

Something postponed immediate response. Filled with both busy people and idlers, one of the city's several *suks*, or market-places, stood before us and, at its nearest corner, a white mosque having an octagonal minaret. Down from this minaret's top fell now the weird cry of the muezzin calling the faithful. It was the moment for evening-prayer.

As if they were a wheat-field swept by a sudden west wind, every man in sight bent low to earth, his white robes flapping. Like all the rest, the Lord Chief Justice of Tripoli turned eastward, as toward Mecca, knelt in the dust and the dirt and, arms extended, thrice prostrated himself devoutly.

He rose with a sort of creaking grunt as if the bending and rising hurt, but this finished in a burst of his cynic laughter:

"Bully or not, your big acquaintance with the crooked shoulder has decided to become a Mohammedan — he and a certain number of his fellow-slaves who are under his influence. Who knows? — Perhaps they long to nestle in the breast of Allah. Perhaps" — the Kaya spoke with soft contemplativeness

145

— "perhaps one argument that moves them toward conversion toward the only religion is the fact that then our faith will terminate their bondage. They will no longer be slaves."

I must have choked over the idea. Anyway, I muttered something about Christians and living up to what you'd been taught to believe in.

"Oh," said Sidi, as if to assure me there was no cause for me to worry. "This Wilson dog offers something of more value than his wretched soul. He understands all about that boat we took: the *Philadelphia*. He has promised to take her out to sea, under Ibrahim Bey's command. She will fly your pretty flag, thus disguising herself, but in that way he can safely approach her late escort and — capture her for Tripoli."

My heart turned over. My brain tried to deny my ears. I could not forbid my tongue from leaping to protest:

"No — no! Not the *Vixen!*"

Yet I felt that he spoke the truth. What was I, here in this barbarian city, save a helpless bondsman that he should not taunt me with a planned deed which I should

146

be utterly unable to prevent?

"Ah, the *Vixen*," he echoed, his mirth composing itself to a bland smile again. "Thank you, fellow; you already prove yourself useful: I had forgotten her name. The *Vixen* it is. She will welcome the *Philadelphia* as one fond sister welcomes another who has been long given up for dead. And then — Thank you again, boy."

CHAPTER XI

PERIL IN THE PANTRY

L ITTLE did I then learn about the trade of a waiter! Stunned by that sinister news, so gleefully given, I staggered after Sidi Mahommed first along arcaded streets, then through the Turkish quarter and so up the terraces to the city's top.

Following my new master, I entered the Kaya's courtyard and his sprawling, white-washed house with one sole desire in my heart: to get through my evening's tasks as soon as might be, in order that, returning to the officers' prison, I could acquaint Captain Bainbridge — though he must prove as helpless as myself — with the dark doing afoot. This was the first news from outside that we had obtained since the beginning of our imprisonment, but it was dire news indeed.

The cook into whose care I was committed proved to be a one-eyed Mussulman whose Spanish equalled mine. He provided water with which to wash, and even turned his back so I dared bathe my swollen feet with impunity. He also gave me a change of clothes — that jacket and those baggy trousers had doubtless lately been worn by the poor servant whose hands were amputated. My own hands hung far below the sleeves, awkwardly big for this Moorish fit.

He turned round at last and surveyed me. For an instant, there was no expression in his solitary eye, then suddenly it gathered a twinkle. The cook poised hands on hips and leaned far backwards. His big mouth opened to let out what would have been a loud guffaw had he risked vocalizing it. He shook in derisive laughter at the picture I made.

Probably I flushed. Certainly I felt the red mount to the roots of my hair. This costume of grimy baggy trousers, the sleeves of the upper part of the rig like the sleeves in a woman's gown, and, finally, the turban without which I should be forbidden the Kaya's presence: it was all like being handed the fool's cap to wear for lessons missed.

Yet my Mussulman-cook was perhaps the least cruel

of my captors, being easy-going except where his own work was involved — and of an exacting disposition, including the everlasting kicks for accompaniment, when he thought it time for me to aid in part of this. He himself doubtless feared the lash and invited no criticism of his department from his superiors; besides, the fate of my predecessor must have been vivid before his memory.

"I will shove the platters prepared through this sliding-door to the pantry, where you will collect them and serve them quick, quick, Boy. The Kaya likes his hot dishes hot, and he likes the others at once, before almost he can clap his hands. You will put this cloth under the dishes — then the hot ones will not burn your fingers. But if they do burn your fingers, still do not drop them — or you will mayhap lose the fingers that were careless."

He gave me other, and minute, instructions, all with their separate threats for negligence; before them my muddled brain whirled dizzily. There was, it appeared, to be a guest tonight. I was to serve Sidi and his guest in the apartment just beyond the pantry. Having completely bewildered and terrified me, the cook gave me a shove — and an extra kick for good measure — and pushed me out of his kitchen and into the cubbyhole that held the dining-room utensils, and me until I should be summoned.

Not from any particular interest in my coming task, but because it was best, I concluded, to learn the lay of the land and lessen the chances of incurring that punishment meted out to the former waiter, or one of the many others suggested by the cook, I opened the heavy serving-door. I peeped into the next apartment and looked around.

Here, under the usual swinging, parti-colored lamps was only a small room, but it looked twice its size because of its white walls and scanty furniture. It contained to be sure some Moorish decoration of delicate stucco arabesque work, but otherwise it contained nothing save a low table, already dressed for the meal, so I had no worry over that. The table was mounted on legs of most intricate workmanship and stood between two divans covered with rugs and heaps of cushions. I was on the tip of stepping in to reconnoitre

151

when I heard another door, from the opposite side, being opened.

Evidently Kaya and his guest were already coming in. I ducked back into the pantry!

Lest the noise attract unfavorable attention, I did not quite shut the portal that shielded my retreat. Instead, I allowed it to hang an unobservable half-inch open, never dreaming, as I did so, that to this would be due my gain of yet further, and equally important, information.

"My friend," I heard Sidi say almost at once, and in his slow silky voice, to the person he had invited for dinner, "if you think I have what-you-call 'threatened' you, it is only because in this court of His Mighty — but mighty stingy — Majesty Yusuf, Conqueror of the Great, Son of the Prophet and Pasha of Tripoli, we all have to fill our purses when and how we can. I speak frankly in my own chambers where I can be sure there is none to overhear."

None to overhear!

He was free of his talk because that service-door was thick and, as he supposed, fastened. Had it been properly in its place — and it was obvious he did not conceive I would dare to open it — no sound could have pierced through short of the brazen gong he was going to beat whenever he required me. However, it gaped that little bit, and so I could listen to every word without seeing either speaker. I gasped in terror at my precarious situation.

Sidi went on:

"I guessed you had not told me all the truth, my friend. I know you well enough to believe you a man of wisdom."

Yet here again he was speaking Spanish! It was unaccountable. Did none in this city, save sovereign and soldiers, talk their native tongue?

There came at last a rasping phrase from the other invisible:

"Since you have found me out, I shall give you half of what I receive for the letter. That is the utmost you can ask."

Hidden as I was, I instinctively sought deeper concealment by pressure against the pantry-wall; for I should have recognized that raucous voice anywhere:

Ventura Gonzales' — Ibrahim Bey's! "The letter" could mean only one thing. To me, there could, besides, be only one letter now in the entire world.

  I had been right in my conjectures, then, that this crafty fellow had kept Secretary Madison's dangerous document from the Pasha in order to dispose of it elsewhere: it looked as if Silverio had all along been the Turk's colleague and had helped me on the chase, thwarting me in the end, only to lure me as far from Cadiz as possible. Now the secret was detected by the even more crafty Kaya, who was not averse to dispensing justice with weighted scales, and whose prompt price for disloyal silence was a goodly share in the prospective spoils.

On every side around me in the pantry rose shelves full of cups and covered dishes elaborately designed: they began to heave up and down as if I were once more on a ship at sea. Should either of those worthies out there become interested in that thin crack between door and frame, and investigate, I was a dead lad!

"Moreover," purred the unctious voice of Sidi, "you will bring back a stamped paper, you understand, stamped and signed, too, wherein the purchaser will state just how much he paid."

The thief complained — whiningly. He would never dare ask for such a document. It was not etiquette; it was unfair. I lost the first part of his remonstrance, but the hoarse conclusion, with its note of offended righteousness, reached me clearly:

"Do you doubt my honesty?"

"As I doubt my own," came the prompt reply with easy assurance. "I presume that your purpose is to go direct to France and deal with Napoleon himself, or with someone close in power to him?"

"That is it — as soon as I have captured the other frigate for His Majesty."

"The *Vixen*, yes. You seem to feel very sure of succeeding in that capture. Do you not fear there may be obstacles?"

Ibrahim Bey laughed raucously: "I am sure to succeed — with this dog Wilson's help — and with Allah's. The sailor is a rascal, but I shall not lose the whip-hand."

"Ah, well, you will know about that enterprise's

termination the day after tomorrow. So shall we all. I hope you are right, for the Pasha counts on it, and he is a child at disappointment. He will be loath to let you leave the country for any other errand — I mean the arrangement about the letter — if you fail. He does not like failures."

"Do I not know? But I shan't be one, never fear. Yet," he added after a moment's pause, "if Kismet should fail me there, nevertheless I would find even another chance to regain the royal favor which the American Captain's version of his capture lost me."

So the Pasha had not altogether believed Ibrahim's boastings!

Sidi said: "Praise be to Allah!"

And the other echoed: "Praise!"

Abruptly, in clanging contrast to the tones of my master, the gong rang. He and his guest were ready to be served.

Could I do it — could I venture in? Nearly fainting, I opened the sliding board into the kitchen and put my head through. The cook at once pushed at me a large metal platter, appallingly hot and full of rice and hashed beef wrapped in vine-leaves — pieces the size of walnuts: *Yalandji Dolmas* they were called, I learned later, and I shall never inhale their aromatic odor again but what I think of that evening.

As I shoved open to its full width the door to the dining apartment, with my platter carefully balanced above the napkin I had fortunately there for protection from the heat, I was a-tremble from head to foot. Sidi reclined on one divan, bulging from comfortable fat; Ibrahim on the other, nervous and thin. The Turk started in amazement.

"What?" he sneered. "You háve one of the American swine here for house-servant. I had thought you a man of prudence."

This was necessarily in Spanish, but Sidi was ready to voice his amusement. "He comes for only a few hours daily. Is that imprudent? Besides, the giant Wilson, whom you champion, showed certain signs of disliking him. I was obliged to take the boy in order to discipline the novice to the religion of Allah. Discipline is good for the soul, even for the new-born Mohammedan soul. Do you not agree?"

157

Ibrahim's black glance roved almost anxiously from me to his host. If he wished to say anything that would be understood, he must reply in Spanish. Whatever he now said, he knew I must understand. He was disconcerted — I knew why — but he asked: "The fellow hasn't heard, has he?"

Sidi rubbed his hands complacently. "What foolish alarms, my friend. Go and look at the door, if you are fearful: it is a heavy door, built at my instructions, against ears that might have to be removed if they heard too much."

The Turk did not examine the door. He decided to show himself contented, though I knew he put another mark against me in his mind. I tried to look deaf and dumb.

Not for one moment throughout that meal did my tension relax, however. There was a soup of a sort the French would call *crème d'orge*, an insipid concoction of barley without meat foundation: when I served it, some of it slopped over my thumb — fortunately not over Sidi's! There was a red fish from the Mediterranean that I nearly dropped, and, not long after, I as nearly

158

dropped the entrée and the roast — *konzorum* — that followed. They had *yonam bayldi* for the next course, and then *yaourt* and fruits and, of course, the sticky, thick coffee those infidels love.

I sighed with relief, thinking I might be free then. Nobody, it appeared, was to guard me to the prison, since my lanky youth and the presence of only the limitless desert and the sea around the city combined to make my escape seem impossible. But the one-eyed cook wanted to profit by his new helper.

"No," he said crossly, when I suggested that my duties for the evening were over. "Wash the dishes. Stay! First serve these bowls."

The bowls were two, each half filled with lime-juice for the eaters to dip their dainty fingers in.

"And then, before washing the dishes, be ready in attendance behind the pantry-door, either until they bid you go or until they arise and go themselves."

So the time dragged on with me ever there, a weary enough lad with aching heels. I thought they would never leave the last ruins of their meal. They talked scarce at all while I was at work, and whenever I left

159

them caution now bade me firmly close the barrier between us.

Only when I cleaned away the final dishes was there any talk of their project, and then it was such as could be of no use to me. Ibrahim's evil eyes did meet mine in one momentary expression of triumph and defiance, on one of my entrances, to be sure, as he restored to the clothing above his breast something that I took to be the precious letter, which might indicate that he habitually carried it about with him for its greater security; but all that Sidi was engaged at was the almost idle drawing of certain lines upon a chance scrap of parchment.

"Call this Marseilles," said he to his guest, who clearly wished me elsewhere, and not in any good place at that. "Then your safest course would not to be the usual one, but by here — and here."

He had neither quill nor crayon. He was making his chart by dipping a proficient index-finger into that lime-juice I had placed before him. The markings faded out almost as soon as they made, and, he and Ibrahim at last rising, the Kaya tossed the already

160

blank parchment among the table-debris.

I got all the service out of the way with such speed as was compatible with the utensils' safety and my still troublesome heels, and cleaned up in the kitchen under sharp criticism from the one-eyed Mussulman — and without the least assistance from him. That scrap of parchment which had been used for charting I tossed into the open fire over which the cook habitually worked, and, as the thing flamed up, I noticed that the heat refreshed to all its pristine clarity the design once drawn there — of no value to me.

However, this was an idle observation, and one I forgot for the time being. I hurried to an end of my job and scuttled, still hobbling somewhat, through the narrow, dark streets to the officers' prison. There I found that Sidi had already calmly informed the native functionaries concerning my new occupation, pleased as much with their agitation over it as ever he had been with Gus Wilson's.

CHAPTER XII

PORTER'S PLOT

THIS jail of mine, as I should have said before, was one wing of an otherwise deserted barracks. An armed guard of five men was always on duty belowstairs, but the captives were allowed much their own way on the floor above. The Tripolitans are a lazy race, and cared more about their games of chance than troubling with us except when we gave definite signs of activity and thereby offered them the pleasant emotion of cruelty. But even cruelty palls, and their hope of ransom from living men kept that pretty well within bounds.

Here, in our quarters, was a long, ill-smelling hall, and off this opened several rooms, their windows securely barred, in which the officers slept, Porter and Bainbridge in cubicles to themselves. I limped to Bainbridge's. He was permitted a dim lamp, which still burned behind its wrought ironwork, for, with the weight he had on

162

him, he slept little.

"You're late," said he. " I was very much exercised about it. We asked the jailors, but either they knew nothing or wouldn't tell — wouldn't say a word to Gibbon, who asked."

Bainbridge had not even heard of the bastinadoing, which I forbore to mention. After all, the soles of my feet promised to be nearly normal by morning, and what were my troubles to his? These last two weeks or so had set their lines upon him. His face was haggard in the shadowy light, and some silver glinted in the cockscomb of his hair.

"Yes, sir." I saluted. "I have been ordered to wait twice a day on Kaya Sidi Mahommed's table." I hated now to add to my commander's depression, but it was my duty to tell him all I had learned. "Our — the *Philadelphia* has been put in condition and is to go out under Ibrahim Bey to capture the *Vixen* — flying the Stars and Stripes."

"What? What?"

I hastened to give him all the details I had, and he listened with a deepening of the new perpendicular

163

wrinkle in his wide brow. When I had finished, he made no comment to me, but knocked twice on the wall beside the floor-mattress serving him for bed.

There was an answering knock, and only a moment thereafter, Porter appeared, sufficiently clothed to make one wonder if he, too, had not been passing sleepless hours, though without the luxury of a light. He closed the door after him and stood against it, pale and thin, but more square-jawed than ever and as iron-willed. He gave me the faintest speculative nod.

"Mr. Porter," said our Captain, "Rowntree brings the first news we've had — and it is not to my fancy." He turned to me: "Repeat it precisely as you told it to me."

I did so, looking from the Captain, running fingers slowly through his unruly curls, to Porter, frowning portentously.

"The first part of it means," Captain Bainbridge interpreted, "that in all probabilities the second of the two ships I brought here will be lost at least indirectly through me — lost like the first — like the *Philadelphia*."

164

"It is more than possible that there has been time for the *Vixen* to guess our fate and leave, sir," said Porter.

"Not at all," the Captain objected. "Smith had his orders. He would continue to obey them till he got specific orders to nullify them, or was relieved from the base. I do not believe he knows our fate. Besides, these pirates are sure the *Vixen's* out there, or they wouldn't so surely plan her capture." For once, Bainbridge's voice broke ever so slightly. "Would to God Smith were gone and had my report with him!"

Porter and I exchanged glances. We both understood what our commander suffered under the thought of how failure to send that report must be construed by Preble — provided even he knew our disaster — as a token of conscious guilt, and I am sure the Lieutenant's heart ached as much as mine. However, the Captain had determinedly refused to send a report including a demand of ransom for us — the only sort of report that would have been allowed through. He now tossed his head as if to toss away personal grief.

"The *Vixen* is on duty!" he declared.

His reasons for this assumption were unanswerable.

Porter asked me:

"Did you hear any date mentioned? That is most important."

"I gathered," I replied, "that the attempt is to be made the day after tomorrow."

In the faint light, two little spots of pink came out on Porter's cheeks, and his thin hands suddenly twitched with eagerness.

"Sir" — he spoke in a sort of suppressed earnestness to his superior officer — "may I venture to remind you of my plan again — and to suggest that it be put in action tomorrow night?"

I cocked my ears and stared. "A plan!" Here was news indeed.

Bainbridge began to pace the room. He looked keenly at his subordinate. He was in shirt and trousers — none too clean, for cleanliness of clothes was a luxury our jailors did not accord even themselves, let alone us. His hands were clasped behind him, and his fingers knotted in and out. "It has barely a chance in the world — barely one chance!"

Porter nodded in agreement: "True. But there is no

166

other chance at all."

"I've risked my men's liberty and lost it," persisted our leader. "Now you propose to me that I should risk their lives on such a foolhardy scheme!"

The pair were friends again, more friends than captain and lieutenant. Therefore Porter urged as a friend, not a subordinate:

"Do you think the men value their life of slavery very high? I'll wager not one of them would not rather risk his life with one single chance of freedom than know he must continue as at present without any hope of release."

Anybody could have seen that Bainbridge was on fire to agree with whatever this plan was that Porter had framed. The commander's long face was aflame, and some of the years that the disaster to the *Philadelphia* had added to his twenty-nine years of reality now visibly dropped away — he anxiously wanted to be persuaded!

Well, I myself had been listening with glowing cheeks. Here was something like! Of the details of the plot I was still as ignorant as could be, but I was content that

167

it was a plot, desperate, too, and for liberty. I fair broke out:

"Oh, sir, the men don't value their present lives! You know I am with one party of them nearly all day long, and you should hear them talk — in whispers of course: I am sure they would do anything if there were the least encouragement offered them. Except for Gus Wilson and his kind, not one of them values his life at a red penny!"

Bainbridge stopped his restless promenade. He made an attempt to be the old salt again and assert his rightful position:

"What's this — what's all this? Who's a cabin boy ex-stowaway to interfere in such matters? Upon my word, you have the assurance to poke your oar into everything, young man!" He was always a bit like that, quick for taking one side or the other violently, but I was less frightened than in the old days. I knew now that he really cared for me, and it would be only a little minute before he would come round and admit the justice of what I said. Sure enough, he was soon smiling a bit, albeit wearily. "Well, well — you've brought

168

grave news tonight, Rowntree; but you must understand that that doesn't entitle you to give advice about it till you're asked for it."

"We all know you can't suppress the boy," grinned Porter, seeing the wind veering in his direction; "but this time he's right."

"In what he tells us about the men? Is that what you mean?"

"Yes, sir."

The desire to be convinced rose still higher in the Captain. He began to pace once more, quick, nervous steps. "I should hope so — of Americans. But the loss of my frigate has made me wary."

It was curious how that misfortune had acted on the two officers, rendering the hothead hesitant and the cautious subordinate bold and daring. Porter squared his ever-square shoulders for a final effort. When he spoke, it was with all his old deliberation, yet with a bran-new force:

"Sir, the loss of the *Philadelphia* supplies the sole argument in my favor, but that argument is overwhelming. The *Vixen* must be close by, as both you and

Sidi declare. Unless we capture the city, Ibrahim Bey and these traitors will undoubtedly capture her."

Bainbridge came up to Porter with firm steps and took his hand:

"We'll try it, Lieutenant."

Just like his former self, the Captain, once having made a decision, dismissed both debate and gratitude. Porter was jubilant, and I was for cheering. But Bainbridge's voice was cold again:

"Details now — details, Mr. Porter. Tomorrow night and the night work-gang is to strike the first blow. None of us officers works after dark: how are those fellows to be told?"

I was so enraptured as to forget his recent admonition and my reputation for interference in affairs over which I had no command.

"Why," said I, "I'm with them. We begin our night-turn tomorrow, and I must join the party right after I've left the raft of dishes in my one-eyed Mussulman's kitchen."

Bainbridge did not call me down this time. Instead, he looked me over with a meditative regard, admitting

170

me of a sudden to a par with Porter:

"I believe you can do it. If you can learn by heart the instructions that must be taken to the men, you shall be given the opportunity — you shall."

"He can," said Porter with a certitude for which I blessed him.

"Try me, sir!" I cried.

"One moment." The Captain tugged at a side-whisker. "Gus Wilson's in that party. We know he's wrong, but we don't know who else is, and there are others. We mustn't let any of those treasonable hounds learn what's to pass or everything is lost. Mr. Porter, how are we to make sure whom we can trust?"

"Bill Ray's true," — I rushed the words at them, nor did I fear reproof at all — "Bill will know which are Wilson's friends because they'll be Bill's enemies."

I had captured full attention and experienced no difficulty in retaining it. Both men listened intently as I rapidly sketched my knowledge of Ray and of Wilson's dislike for him. My hearers, thoroughly convinced, proceeded to make me learn, letter for letter, the entire plot. It was to be my mission to carry to my

171

fellow night-workers next evening the orders for the execution of the first move in this.

Was anything more desperate ever devised, with a city full of native, pitiless rabble against us, and even some of our own men disloyal? I do not wonder that the once impetuous Bainbridge had hesitated: only desperation won his consent — and, on the other side, nothing except desperation moved Porter in the planning of it or maintained him through the urging. Yet what could prisoners devise except the desperate? In brief, here it was:

The night-work was carried on near the Pasha's castle. Those whom we trusted among the nocturnal slaves, therefore, were suddenly to revolt at one o'clock in the morning, every armed guard being assaulted barehanded by a couple of our old crew, when Ray should pass the word. It was of course all to be done as noiselessly as possible, but a certain degree of noise would raise no comment in the city, being put down to the usual personal brawls of Bedouins and the outlaws from the desert.

With the arms thus procured, the self-emancipated

172

Americans were to divide into two squadrons, of which one was to overcome the warders of the officers' prison, release the officers and run with them to the castle, while the other squadron would have gone straight thither.

Inside the royal walls, Dr. Cowdery would have so arranged, as the Pasha's physician, that his self-centred patient should require night-attendance. The medical-man would be leaving at the appointed hour, and the gate would be opened for him. Our men would rush in; the Pasha and his family would be seized — the castle immediately put in a state of defense.

Well, we should have the fat Tripolitan monarch for our hostage — and the castle's guns commanded the city. It would be a splendid advantage for us, and, if there were then any question of ransom, it would have to be the other way round!

I am no hand at either poetry or yet the dialect of Caledonia. Nevertheless, there died in 1796 a democratic Scotch poet named Burns whose works are already becoming popular to the readers of our country, and I mind me having heard that he wrote something

173

like this:

> "The best laid plans o' mice and men
> Gang aft aglee" —

Those words come back to me as I reach this stage of my history.

CHAPTER XIII

INVISIBLE INK

THE existence of prisoners anywhere is either one of dull monotony or one in which hope and despair succeed each other so rapidly that it is small wonder madness often drops a mental curtain. With war prisoners, the case is much the same as with out-and-out criminals so far as the result is concerned, though we were the prisoners of a horde of international bandits of the high seas, who had no higher motive for their actions than loot and the right of might. What came of Porter's impetuous plan, his intellectual struggle with Bainbridge — and what came of the effort that the latter made to risk once more, and on such a thin chance, the lives of his men?

Just this:

Four o'clock of the morning was the hour when the officers were usually summoned to march out of jail for their day's work — a sleepy, shivery hour. On this

175

day, you may be sure that, for the first time, none wanted to lie abed. The chief plotters had wakened all the others betimes in order to acquaint them of what they might expect when another sun rose, and our quarters were abuzz with suppressed whispers.

Since my party of the crew were to go on night-duty that evening, and I was not to be able to join them until after the late meal of Sidi Mahommed, I had received word to remain indoors at least until the Kaya's mid-day mealtime. But every one of my prison-mates was ready — everyone sharing my enthusiasm, was on tip-toe to get through with his toil with as little reprimand-ing as possible, so that he might bend his energies toward the night's revolt.

Four o'clock of the morning — but the chief jailor, contrary to his custom, failed to appear, noisy and brutal, in that upstairs hall where we were gathered awaiting him. We tried to show ourselves outwardly as sleepy and dull for work as usual.

For once did he oversleep? Had some gleam of kind-ness entered his black soul?

We waited — at first unsuspiciously, then impatiently, and finally with growing fears. The North African sun was already high. The curious cries of Moors and Jews bustling to the bazars rose from below. A long caravan of camels in from the desert ambled along the dusty street below, shrieked at by children who brandished whips with the cruelty of their seniors. But within our barracks nothing happened.

We were consumed with restlessness. Porter suggested to our chief:

"Perhaps something has gone wrong with your Geneva, sir."

We knew in our hearts it was not so this time, and Bainbridge answered shortly:

"Nothing ever goes wrong with my Geneva!"

This was in 1803, remember, and Luther Goddard, of Shewsburg, Massachusetts, did not manufacture the first American watch until 1809. In those days, because the French-Swiss were the great watchmakers, and Geneva was their great city, with most of the watch-making headquarters, people called any watch a "Geneva" just as, nowadays, the name "Havana" stands for any cigar. Not everybody was lucky enough

177

to own a watch, even when there were no pirates about
to despoil him of one, but Bainbridge alone among us
had managed, as Captain and therefore to be respected
slightly above his fellows by the Tripolitan rabble, to
save his timepiece when the pirates searched us aboard
the *Philadelphia*.

He was profoundly proud of that cumbersome chronometer because it had come down to him from a
grandfather and was, by its inner mark, plainly of
Swiss make. Still, having learned somewhat of such
matters, I should say that this one must have been
constructed before Le Roy and Earnshaw began using
unequal expansion of the rim-metals to diminish inertia: the very heat of a wearer's body would affect
that balance-wheel's hair-spring, and when I was cabin
boy on the frigate, I had frequent opportunity to note,
by comparison with the sun, both the machine's faults
and how Bainbridge's affection condoned them: it
might have been a pampered favorite-child of his whose
sins the fond parent would not even recognize to himself.

However, it remained here all that we slaves had to

178

go by. We were glad enough to have its partial correctness for guidance.

"Could a warder have overheard any of our talk?" wondered somebody — a boyish midshipman named Bernard Henry, I remember even now it was.

"They would never have understood it if they had heard us," Jim Gibbon, another young middy, reminded him.

Bainbridge addressed the ragged, unshaven company grouped around him, while Gibbon stood guard against our being discovered in seeming conspiracy:

"It is now exactly half-past four, gentlemen. A delay like this has never occurred before. If we are not summoned by a quarter to five, I shall institute some sort of inquiry."

Four forty-five arrived, and no chief jailor with it.

We looked at one another in consternation. Our Captain picked out the purser, Keith Spence, a man who had sailed the Mediterranean seas many a time before and had, of us all, the best smattering of the languages spoken along their coasts.

"Go below, Mr. Spence," said Bainbridge. "See

179

what you can learn."

"Yes, sir." Spence, perhaps the most disreputable-looking of us all, gave a snappy salute and disappeared.

Again we waited. In three minutes, our envoy was back with a gloomy face:

"Only one of them there in his grimy glory," said he, "and the locks turned on him as well as us. No hint of food, which he seemed to think I was looking for. I could get only one thing out of the son of a seacook, sir. He finally said that all outside work has been suspended for two days."

"All work suspended for two days?" frowned Bainbridge, pulling his long nose thoughtfully.

Our hearts sank. This was the death-knell of Porter's plot!

We could only conclude that somebody who comprehended our temper, since not our tongue, feared we would learn of the designs against the *Vixen* and be driven to some such desperate remedy as that toward which we had in fact aspired. I guessed Wilson for the guilty one, since he had seen me taken into Sidi's service and was probably aware, from his own conversations with the Kaya, how careless of speech that dignitary could be. On the other hand, Ibrahim Bey himself might have dropped a word of warning with the authorities.

One must live a long life before he will ever see men more disappointed than were the *Philadelphia's* young officers! The event had checked them from an adventure which would almost certainly have cost their lives, and they were as unhappy as schoolboys denied a once-promised picnic. Like a person utterly put to shame, Porter deserted and shut himself in his own room, and Bainbridge, for all his early hesitation, retired in little better case to the comfortless quarters assigned to him.

Yet I am wrong in implying that only bafflement and chagrin resulted from the scheme, for in me there arose a reaction that stimulated my wits. This unexpected obstacle had been too sudden and quiet to make me believe it without possibility of surmounting. I sought a solution every whichway, and out of the confusion an idea came to me of the sort to stun discretion. It drove me pell-mell to my Captain's door.

"Come in," he muttered, answering my knock — and

when he saw who it was he was too crippled in spirit to scold. "Be quick, though. I've no heart for chatter, Martin — be quick."

"Sir," said I, standing at my straightest, as if delivering the message of some superior officer, "since all of you, officers and men, are to be kept behind closed doors until after this expedition is launched against the *Vixen*, I can't deliver the message you designed and that I learned. But, despite the prohibition against all the rest of us, I think I shall be expected to wait on Sidi Mahommed's table twice today. In that case, there is another message I can bear for you."

"What do you mean?" He regarded me fixedly, as I stood there at attention.

"Tonight, after the Kaya's evening meal, I needn't come back at all."

"Needn't come back at all?"

"I can just quietly steal to the harbor and look for an empty boat, and I can row out to sea and perhaps find the *Vixen* myself, and if I do — oh, Captain Bainbridge, don't you see: there is still time to warn her to get her out of the way!"

He started. Fire flashed in his eyes. Then it died, and he shook his head.

"No, no," he said. "You are a hare-brained lad — a good, brave lad, and loyal, but hare-brained. It is impossible."

I was undismayed. I went right on: "And I can tell Captain Smith all that has happened. I can tell him about the men, and how the Sultan's made us all slaves, and how it's not your fault and —".

"Sh!" He raised a forbidding hand.

Nevertheless, determined that my proposition was wise and feasible, I urged it upon him with all the force I had in me: "Aye, and I should tell her to go back to Gib for reënforcements, and it might come out all right, sir. Won't you please let me try?"

The Captain could not help but see what my idea, carried out successfully, would mean, but he was all for resisting me:

"It is comforting to have further proof of your loyalty — touching, too — but that is too wild a design — too wild."

"It isn't half so wild as Lieutenant Porter's design, sir."

"Too risky. Too risky."

"He would have risked all our lives. Mine risks only mine — and that not very much. If I can't find a loose boat, of course I won't attempt it, whereas if I do find one — "

"You are too young! Why, you're only — "

There was no need for him to remind me:

"I'm scarcely any younger than your youngest midshipman, sir — and inches taller."

He was pacing the chamber again, hands behind him, as he paced it some hours since before Porter and me together — as he so often paced it with the same sharp turns he always made on the bridge of his boat. "I have no right to venture your life," he objected. "It is different from the others': you know that you are not officially in the Navy."

"Sir, it is not you who venture my life; I'm the one who does that. I volunteer, sir — and I hope to be in the Navy very soon."

"By Jove, you deserve to be!" He stopped in front of me, looking me up and down. I tried to continue immobile, but an involuntary grin swept my face.

He was relenting a little, too: "The thing just might
be done — with luck and a compass. You can read a
compass?"

"Yes, sir."

"There's a compass set in the back-case of my Geneva. And Smith's order's were definite. Preble
wouldn't have got to him to change them. I know
within twenty miles where the *Vixen*'d be at this very
moment."

Seeing how the man was wavering, I clinched my plea:

"Besides, sir, this way you can write your report,
without the ransom embargo. I'll take it out with me
and deliver it."

Now, I do not mean to insinuate that Captain Bainbridge consented to let me peril myself for the sake of
the report which could be his only justification in the
affair of the *Philadelphia* — his only hint, too, of how
perhaps his men might otherwise be rescued. It was his
duty to draw up some such statement and to dispatch it
at the first opportunity, and I know, too, that just now,
he thought most of all about saving the *Vixen* and those
aboard her. Still, when so much else was in my favor,

the addition of that grain turned the scales.

Further dissent there was, but weaker and weaker. In the end, bursting with elation, I had my way.

He handed his big Geneva to me — I hoped the compass was more reliable than the watch part — and soon, before a rickety table bearing the pens and parchment sent by the Pasha, he fell to at that report, setting me at the door to warn him of intrusion.

"I must write this," said he, pondering, "in such terms as can give no valuable information, should it happen to fall into the enemy's hands. And yet I must try to make it complete."

He was by no means so sure as was I that my attempt would succeed. The *Philadelphia* was now our enemies' ship, sufficiently overhauled to be seaworthy; she possessed certain faults in construction and equipment of which only her proper officers were aware, and some of these faults might be mentioned in extenuation of what had happened. Also, it might be well, in case of an encounter, that the Americans be made cognizant of these in order to take advantage of them. But Bainbridge did not want to be in the position of giving her

186

new masters the very data that would equally arm them.

I understood — and had my second inspiration for that morning.

"Write with invisible ink, sir!" I suggested, bursting with the idea.

I have said that our jailors' only liberality was in the provision of fruits. On the table here where Bainbridge had already started to write, there now stood a large platter of limes, and I had happened to recall what resulted to Sidi Mahommed's idle chart for Ibrahim, when it was thrown into the kitchen-fire.

I rapidly told him.

The Captain would not believe his ears: "Can it be so?"

I remembered that Jim Gibbon, the middy, had found a dropped tinder-box on the quay and prized it highly ever since.

"May I call Gibbon?" I asked. "I believe we can prove it, sir."

He brought in the box at once, and struck fire, while we sacrificed bits of paper scrawled over with lime-juice to the flame. For an hour we worked, in order to make sure, daring to give only the smallest necessary amount of parchment for our supply was of the scantiest. Then, convinced, the Captain set to work to write.

With a clean quill, and a solution of lime-juice that Gibbon and I prepared, he wrote the report with as great speed as he could. Ere its final sentences had been penned, all the earlier used sections of the parchment gave an appearance as innocent of text as before that quill had touched them.

Midday arrived, and with it a summons that dispelled the final doubt of my opportunity: I was brusquely directed to repair to Sidi's. Nobody feared freedom of movement in a mere cabin boy turned landwaiter.

Tonight I should go again to the Kaya's. Then, through the dark and tortuous streets, I would try to lose myself from the pirates and start my desperate attempt to regain my own freedom and to deliver my commander's message to the Captain of the *Vixen*.

CHAPTER XIV

STRANGE WATERS

WHEN you recollect what lay ahead of me, you will not marvel that I waited with throbbing impatience to undertake it. Somehow I must manage to escape from my slavery in the city of Tripoli, that first — then somehow get out to sea — and then somehow make my way to the *Vixen* and warn her of the pirates' plot for her capture. The hours danced with interminable fretfulness between my return from Sidi's in the mid-afternoon to the jail and my summons to go back to the Kaya's house after sunset to serve his evening meal.

But that sunset — blood-red — faded at last, as we all watched it with trepidation through our prison-bars, and the darkness descended calm and clear. The stars hung low, like all Mediterranean stars, and bright, but not too bright. What wind there was turned out to be a shore-wind and likely, Captain Bainbridge said, to hold.

189

Another thing in my favor was that there was an early moon, and an early moon meant an early setting.

I had the precious Geneva and its compass in my baggy breeches' pocket and Bainbridge's apparently blank parchment inside my shirt and against my breast. The middy who owned the tinder-box gave me that almost indispensible instrument. All things looked auspicious.

I own to enjoying my departure from the prisoners' common-room. Minor officers — yet real enough officers in the United States Navy — wrung my hands and wished me luck, and frankly envied me, for, now that the first plan was impossible of execution, everybody had been informed of the new one afoot. Lieutenant Porter thrust out his square jaw and said he had always believed in me from the day he first saw me, red-faced and ragged and dirty, being towed by Bill Ray to the Captain's cabin, and he told me he was as sure of me now as then; and, last of all, Bainbridge drew me to the door:

"I don't know if I am doing right," he said, looking down his long nose. "Mind, I'm not doing this for you,

however much you want to think it; for, if I owe your
uncle something, I owe our country more, and you're
the only one of the lot of us who can possibly carry this
scheme out. Frank Rowntree would agree — he'd
agree. So go now, and God bless you — God bless and
speed you, boy."

My chest swelled with pride — and made the parchment crinkle a bit — while my heart thumped from
apprehension; yet neither betrayed me utterly. I
nodded casually to the warders; I pretended not to heed
the curious glances bestowed by white-robed and turbaned Moors upon a "dog of a Christian" as I picked
my course through those narrow, ill-smelling streets —
under the arcades — along the walled gardens, whose
barriers failed to hide the tops of tamarisk, mastic and
pistachio trees — and so at last beside the octagonal-
towered Pasha Mosque, which used to be a Spanish
church in the days of the Sixteenth Century when King
Ferdinand and the Knights of St. John occupied this
city.

Suspiciously enough I was admitted to the pleasant
court-yard within and so made my way to the kitchen.

191

The one-eyed cook inclined toward a sort of scornful friendliness, perhaps grateful for my having relieved him of some of his own work the night before. His workshop was incalculably dirty underfoot, but his one good eye was not inimical.

As he prepared for the forthcoming meal, droning a monotonous song all the while, I went in and out of the kitchen and through to the divaned dining room to prepare for the diners. He stood with his back to me, and on my second entrance, he called out something that evidently invited me to approach.

I stood still, not quite understanding. Whereupon, in as casual manner as he might toss it to a dog, he threw a morsel of something unexpectedly over his shoulder in my general direction. Then he pirouetted around to see if I had caught it.

That first time, I certainly had not. He scowled, kicked the object out of the room and re-presented his back to me. The second time I returned, I was ready for him and by good luck nabbed the morsel hurled, in mid-air.

Immediately he gave me a vigorous and approving

192

sign of his head and a wide grin that showed all his teeth and the very roof of his mouth. Silently his shoulders shook with pleased laughter.

The only disadvantage to this method of my getting my dinner was that the cook was erratic in his choice of tidbits and black with anger if I did not at once eat what I caught. As he began this shower of food with something I think they called Turkish Delight, a jelly-like sweet powdered with sugar or flour, and ended it with lumps of greasy meat, I ate in a somewhat topsy-turvy order. Nevertheless, I was glad for food of any sort, and in any order, remembering that I should dare to take scant time at the end of the Kaya's repast to satisfy my hunger.

Sidi Mahommed this time dined with two uninteresting native officials, who meant nothing to me, and whom I cared not if I ever saw again; for once, the language was not Spanish, so that, even if I had wished, I should not have been able to understand what they said. Their host — I divined it was because of his complacency over his shrewd bargain with Ibrahim Bey — gave me easy smiles that were sometimes totally amical,

193

at others scarce more than half cruel. When my hand shook in offering *Rôti Kouzoum*, a little lamb over-roasted on a spit and served whole and sizzling from the fire, he only said in his almost soothing tones:

"You are still a novice and therefore nervous. Those who serve must learn never to tremble: it gives me no pleasure when I eat. But that will pass: it will pass. An hour's beating — that is the quickest cure for nervousness, eh?"

His jocoseness which would yesterday have terrified me out of my wits, rather strengthened than weakened my purpose today. Besides, there was no time for a beating; I must not tremble again. Fortunately, the succeeding dishes were less cumbersome, and my sole accident occurred in the pantry itself, where I upset a platter of fruits and had to scurry around for oranges that rolled out of reach and replace them and the dates rapidly to prevent detection: there was no time to wipe off the dust they gathered, and, to tell the truth, I felt small pity for my master and the possible effect of dirt collected from the floor on his anatomy. The guests talked excitedly and at length, and I thought they

194

would never go, but after I had cleared off the deserted table and washed its last dish, I was quite calm.

"Buenas noches," I said cheerfully to the cook as he let me out.

"Buenas noches," said he — and, in half-embarrassed manner, added "Señor."

Then, as if he would counteract his momentary politeness, he gave a hissing, whispered summons. I wheeled about. From the light-defined open Moorish doorway, he was tossing me a final gift. I barely caught it, a large hunk again of that same Turkish Delight with which he had commenced his shower of food. I stuffed it in a pocket of my baggy trousers.

Once more I was in the open air of night. The silent streets wound slightly down hill ahead. From behind blew a breeze off the desert. Somewhere before me and below lay the harbour — and beyond that, the wide Mediterranean. I could smell the purer sea air on the farther side of the thousand city odors.

Toward that purer scent I turned. I was unarmed — my fellow-prisoners had had no arms to give me, naturally — yet somehow I was not really afraid, and I moved on with elation for my project. If I could only succeed!

Few people were abroad — respectable Tripolitans are early to bed, even if they are not healthy, wealthy and wise, — and, whenever the shadow of anybody did distantly appear, it could be avoided by a lively dive into one or other of the scores of crossways that bisected those slightly downward-tending roads. I had but to lie low for a couple of minutes, then pursue the general declivity and the scent of the water. If most of these fetid thoroughfares were unknown to me, if there was something eerie about these endless rows of silent, flat houses and blank walls bearing blind gates firmly fastened against marauders, all I needed to do was to keep a wary eye roving up and down, to right and to left, and then choose, out of all the lone descents, that descent which looked the most lonely.

At last I thus arrived near to water-level and peered about me. The way I had elected for this portion of my journey led through that Roman Triumphal Arch I have already mentioned: it is of sculptured marble, but the blocks held together by iron bands, and a coffee-house, somewhat disreputable, has been hollowed out of its right side. Lights advertised the resort as still active, and so did laughter, so I made a large circuit and struck the harbor-edge itself only a full quarter of a mile eastward.

Still fortune favored me, though time, I knew, was passing all too fast. Everything was as still as an empty cellar about that particular stretch of shore — everything quiet, too, on the crescent-shaped body of water except where the gleam of distant torches told me that the finishing-touches were being given the *Philadelphia* to make her ready for tomorrow night's nefarious enterprise under pirate control. Best of all, among the many rowboats beached here, the very first I came upon was not even so much as tied up — just carelessly waiting me — and she had her oars aboard.

Snap!

I jumped back. But the noise's cause was at once explained by common-sense. It was no person: I had stepped on a brittle bit of sun-dried wood long since washed up by the water.

That boat wasn't heavy. She was, on the contrary,

somewhat dangerously light for my adventure, and I might have found, with searching, one with a sail. Nevertheless, I took her gladly, being at last too hurried for farther search. Without the least difficulty, I shoved her off. The sea was chill to my heated flesh as I waded in and crawled aboard. It must have been about one o'clock in the morning, a full hour since I had left Sidi Mahommed's, when I began rowing out, through the harbor, toward the Mediterranean proper.

I pulled.

And I pulled.

And I pulled!

If my days of servile labor on the fortifications of Tripoli had done nothing else for me, they had at least hardened temperament and muscles, and fortunately Sidi had saved me from being too severely bastinadoed: I had quite forgotten my heels in other worries. I had always been what the English sailors at Cadiz called "strongish": now I could honestly be put down as really strong. Well, it was necessary!

I passed boldly under the *Philadelphia's* lee, because that frigate lay in what I deemed my most direct course.

A voice — the voice, of course, of somebody on watch, hailed me. Its tone was half jocular, and I made what I hoped sounded like a jocular noise in response, but one that, while containing the intonation of the natives contained no actual words. It sufficed; I was suffered to go on.

With steady, not too enervatingly swift pulls, I made as directly as I could guess due north. Over my left shoulder was blotched against the sky the silhouette of Tripoli's citadel, which, like the Grand Mosque, dates from the Spanish occupation; over my right ran the pale line of the forts at that end of their pentagon, with Tripoli a great, straggling mass behind. The rest of the whole universe was rippling black water and star-spangled purple sky. The harbor had been like glass, but soon an almost imperceptible swell warned me of my approach to the harbour's outer rim. Then only I dared to use my tinder-box and consult the compass borne by Captain Bainbridge's Geneva.

And then: "*Boom-m-m-m!*"

A shot from the citadel rolled out to sea after me, heavy and dour.

I first thought the light I had struck must have betrayed me, but the guns were too cumbersome to answer so suddenly: I knew this could not be so. The truth would be bad enough, but not quite that bad: my absence past a reasonable hour had disquieted the warders at the officers' prison; they had sought me vainly at the house of Sidi Mahommed and through the return-alleys. Where was I? They were all asking that, and, finally truly alarmed, asking it officially.

I was, therefore, now known to have escaped. Well, my direction was not yet detected, and there would be no information got out of the prisoners in those barracks concerning me!

"*Boom-m-m-m!*"

Again that dismal rumble. It was the general alarm sounded to indicate the escape of a man held for ransom. I was worth just so much in American dollars and cents, and they meant to find me.

My pulls became swifter. If I had pulled hard when I set out from the shore, how hard I pulled now, with no heed to the noise of my oars. I met the open water — or it met me. Swells, now very considerable, tossed my stolen boat, which rose and fell with them at thrill-in-spiring angles; spray splashed my face. What had the compass said? — I pulled!

After a while, a dull third gun fired — from farther away.

I paused now long enough in my rowing to look back-ward. Yes — there were bobbing lights all along Trip-oli's lengthy waterfront: torches. Some troops might be sent to scour the nearer desert: here would come boats, more wisely pointed, to search the neighboring sea. It was very well to consider this mere cabin boy harmless while he stayed within his bounds — and bonds; but escaped, and at this crucial moment, he as-sumed a disproportionate importance even beyond the important one of his own personal ransom. It mightn't be forever before they guessed the truth.

The breeze dropped.

I don't know how long I kept on rowing, but until I was numb from it. It seemed many hours, and it must undoubtedly have been several, but my excitement was still too high to make me accurate about that. I was in good physical shape, yet at last first the calves of my legs began to ache and then the muscles of my upper-arms. If only, back there, I had delayed long enough to pick out a boat that carried canvas! The ache grew worse — monotonous.

By this time I was, long since, well out at sea. I had not dared to strike another light. My one purpose was to pursue that generally northerly course, as Bainbridge had directed, and so I put my boat head-on to the waves, thinking that they would be moving inland with the tide, and utterly forgetting that the Mediterranean is tideless.

There came the cold that precedes the dawn. There came hunger from the unusual exercise — and I was ever a hungry person! — and I ate that wretched, thirst-provoking Turkish Delight: I had been too agitated in Sidi Mahommed's pantry to provide myself with such fragments of food as passed through my hands on their way back from diners to kitchen. Worst of all, out here in the salt air and in the very punishment of that sweet — perhaps as much first from suggestion as anything else — there came thirst. More and more my muscles revolted. I had to rest my oars.

Wearily now, I looked backward — or was it backward? The shore was swallowed up, at all events, and no lights gleamed; but here loomed a dark shape — a big dark shape — from the direction in which the coast should be. Was it a ship? Was it possible that the *Philadelphia* was already under way?

I looked forward — a vast world of darkness and mystery.

On my left, however, what should be the horizon began to acquire a cast of faint gray. The morning would soon break. First, my heart rejoiced at that; next, my intelligence warned me that, if I were indeed being pursued, daylight must infallibly discover me to my enemies. They might overlook a little boat like mine in the dark — but in the sun, never; and those guns and torches had told me that the pirates were in no mind to relinquish pursuit without giving it a full trial.

I laid hold of the oars again.

To what purpose against a full-rigged vessel — if, in fact, that big, dark shape which I had seen over-shoulder was a vessel? Yet, if I did not succeed, what was to become of all those men back there? Would they be separately punished in vengeance for my escape? I was desperately afraid they would.

I looked again. Though ever so little, the skies were certainly brightening; and the thing behind me showed itself ghostly, yet clear: a ketch — a ketch undeniably like the *Mastico!*

The *Philadelphia*, as I thought a little more rationally, must lack some hours of being ready. It simply could not be the *Philadelphia*. So, perhaps, on the discovery of my escape and the final obvious conjecture as to its purpose, the *Mastico* had hurriedly taken her place, prepared to attack, perforce and at once, the *Vixen* openly. When he bore news that would warn their enemy and lead to that enemy's flight, the cabin boy became as dangerous to the pirates as any admiral: he must be stopped. Of course, if they caught me first, their other action would be unnecessary.

I rowed. — How I rowed, though now I knew I was really moving slowly from lax muscles.

My legs were all wrong, but I kept on. My arms and back were breaking apart, but I kept on anyhow. As for my head —

204

My head went crazy. If that ketch was visible to me,
I must be just as visible to her lookout. My identity
would never be doubted — I should be overhauled and
retaken — soon — and all my fine purpose would have
been of no avail. Senselessly, lacking hope now and
losing all feel of the direction I was taking, I just rowed.

Then the sun bounded over the horizon — suddenly.
One minute I was in a kindly grayness with pale stars
overhead, seen as through a lady's veil; the next, and
the dazzling maker of full day dominated all the
heavens. Everywhere around swayed gently a calm
blue sea and sky, though with a hint above of wind-
clouds southeastwards, those wicked winter clouds
which bear the gales from the Great Desert. Behind
me, ominously gaining with my every heart-beat, came
that ketch straight toward me. — And ahead?

Was that another sail, faint as a fairy cloud, out
there?

It looked like a brig's canvas, and the Moors did not
venture to sail that type of ship. It danced before my
straining gaze — it was gone. What with exhaustion,
disappointment and genuine fright, I pronounced my-

self delirious.

I gave the ketch a fresh glance: she was ever much nearer. I altered my course: she altered hers. I changed mine again: she changed hers. She was frankly chasing me.

It was idiotic to pull any more. It was all as good as over!

I looked this way and that in final desperation. No help.

I thought I saw the phantom brig again in what I took to be a new quarter of mingled sea and sky. Again it vanished as mockingly as any creature of hallucination.

And yet — oh, I was crazy! — letting my useless oars drop overboard, I rose in my rocking boat. I tore off the jacket of that waiter at Sidi Mahommed's whose hands his master had had amputated. I waved it high over my head — at nothingness — at the spot where had disappeared my second spectre of a non-Moorish craft. Well knowing that no shout from my parched throat could carry any appreciable distance, I nevertheless shouted at the top of what remained of my lungs.

Even as I did so, a huge shadow fell upon me, and a

roar of churning water burst upon my ears. I turned my head. That roar was the sea's as she was cloven by the ketch: that shadow was the shadow of the ketch's prow.

She was upon me!

With a splintering crash, she struck my tiny rowboat full amidships.

CHAPTER XV

A QUEER WELCOME

A S MY cockleshell broke and went under, the force of the impact threw me far backward and to one side: I was no more than a straw in a hurricane. Yet I must somehow have retained some instinctive wit and puny strength. I found myself *not* drowning in the waves. Almost as perilously, I was spinning in mid-air and hanging on for dear life to a rope that had been tossed to me from the poop of the ketch in the moment when the smash occurred.

My arms didn't ache now: they didn't dare! And I could hear my heart go thump-thump-thump. Spray splashed me, but I was wet — I realized later — only to my knees. I had caught the rope high and, although bashed against the ship's side, gone up a few pulls hand-over-hand.

Faces lined the rail above there, bending toward me. I couldn't make out what sort, for I was dizzy through and through and did not much concern my whirling brain with them: I must meet disaster as bravely as I could, that was my main thought, that and regret that my expedition for my Captain and brave Porter and good old Ray, who'd been so kind to me, was ending so unpropitiously.

Cries rang out. I couldn't distinguish words. Then people began to haul.

I managed to help, bracing my feet against the damp side. It seemed to take a long time. However, it was over at last. I was pulled over the rail and sprawled on the deck — safe for the moment.

In a sort of dream, I seemed to hear a rollicking sailor's voice from high up in the rigging chanting familiar words in my own tongue, and I knew I ought to pinch myself out of what must be delirium. I never heard the "Bay Of Biscay O!" without a lift of my spirits, even now in my present daze.

It sounded cynically reassuring:

> "Loud roar'd the dreadful thunder,
> The rain a deluge show'rs;
> The clouds were rent asunder,

By lightning's vivid pow'rs.
  The night both drear and dark;
Our poor devoted bark;
    Till next day,
    There she lay,
      In the bay of Biscay O!

Now dash'd upon the billows,
  Our op'ning timbers creak —
Each fears a wat'ry pillow,
    None stops the dreadful leak,
      To climb the slippery shrouds,
      Each breathless seaman crowds,
        As she lay,
        Till the day
          In the bay of Biscay O!

At length the wish'd for morrow,
  Broke through the hazy sky;
Absorbed in silent sorrow,
    Each heav'd a bitter sigh!
      The dismal wreck to view,
      Struck horror to the crew,
        As she lay,
        On that day,
          In the bay of Biscay O!

A QUEER WELCOME

> Her yielding timbers sever,
>   Her pitchy seams are rent;
> When heav'n all bounteous ever,
>   Its boundless mercy sent —
>   A sail in sight appears,
>   We hail her with three cheers!
>   Now we sail
>   With the gale,
>   From the bay of Biscay O! "

The finish of the song came faint and far off, and everything passed from my consciousness in a sound of roaring. I knew nothing more until somebody held a flagon of water to my lips, pressing me to drink. That revived me. Then somebody else commanded in no tone to be disregarded:

"Get up, yo' young houn' dawg!"

More in answer to the voice than the words, I staggered somewhat erect — and immediately rubbed my eyes. The things I saw appeared like crazy continuation of those insistent visions which had fuddled me in my stolen boat.

I stood, half swaying, in the centre of a ring of staring men, much as on that first occasion of my boarding the

211

Mastico, but there was now a vital — an inexplicable — difference. Excepting one, which plainly showed itself Italian, among all the staring countenances surrounding me this morning, the only brown skins were weather-bronzed. Here were no Turks in disguise — no bearded and turbaned Tripolitans. The officer who had spoken with authority possessed the soft drawl owned only by the natives of some of our own Southern States — and he wore the welcome uniform of a United States Naval Lieutenant. I've seldom met a more gladsome sight or heard a sweeter sound.

Another officer whispered something to him.

"Why," he said as in answer, and having a good squint at me from top to toe, "I believe yo're a white man after all!"

He evinced as much astonishment at my color as my gaze betrayed at his. It was no occasion to remind him that the Moors also belong to the Caucasian family: besides, in my eyes, they will always remain black for their deeds as I had learned to know them in Tripoli. Instead, I replied:

"I'm not only a white man, sir. I belong to the

United States of America, too."

"Ho, ho!" said he, twinkling and looking me over well while I in turn considered him. Of course, I had no inkling of his identity and, knowing, should have then been no better informed; but he was a figure to be looked at intently.

There exists a well-known portrait of Stephen Decatur that the great Gilbert Stuart painted about seven years before its subject's death in his duel with Commodore Barron, but, dashing as that makes him, it is not half so spirited and handsome — at least to my mind — as he was this day when I first saw him, and as he remained throughout his command of the Frigate *Intrepid*. Barely twenty-four, and very boyish with it all, yet he combined with an exuberant manner and talkative disposition the easy mien of a gentleman and what I have always held to be the carriage proper to an officer. A keen eye he had and a quick-tempered one, too, but as kind as brave when he liked — a slightly aquiline nose and a merry mouth — untroubled by worries. His side-whiskers were just grown, and he was still vain of them; of his curling hair, one lock, like that

213

of the little girl in the nursery-rhyme, hung

> "Right down the middle of the forehead."

"An American?" he now repeated in the speech of that Maryland where, I later learned, he had been born and bred. "Egad, we chased yo' fo' a Tripoli pirate-scout! If English is yo' native lingo, why didn't yo' answer our hails?"

That was a period when the whole Navy indulged in extravagances of costume allowable only under loose regulations; but some observers might have thought this representative unduly exceeded his fellows. His coat-lapels flared extraordinarily, flashing with gold-braid, and the wide exposure of his shirt-front was frilled to perfection, though even then I wondered how he could find servants aboard to cater to it. Coming from a prison-life among officers in rags, ill-treated, underfed, I noted those things, and the curl which crowned them. Into my mind rushed the query: Could this be a mere dandy — or a "maccaroni," as we then still called it. No, doubts were banished, and my admiration for my rescuer was sealed by the air of true gallantry and iron determination which enveloped such

214

A QUEER WELCOME

trifles with him and gave them honest value.

"I didn't hear any hails, sir," said I. Most like, I had been first too fatigued and then too scared to hear them! But as for *Biscay Bay*, that, I now knew, was real; for once more there descended that sailorman's voice from among the rigging, less rollicking, but clear as a buoy-bell:

> "In a clime, whose rich vales feed the marts of the world,
>   Whose shores are unshaken by Europe's commotion,
> The Trident of commerce should never be hurl'd,
>   To incense the legitimate powers of the ocean.
>   But should PIRATES invade,
>   Though in thunder array'd,
>   Let your cannon declare the free charter of TRADE.
>
> For ne'er shall the sons of Columbia be slaves,
> While the earth bears a plant or the sea rolls its waves.

Should the Tempest of War overshadow our land,
  Its bolts could ne'er rend Freedom's temple asunder;
For unmoved at its portal would WASHINGTON stand,
  And repulse with his breast the assaults of its thunder
        His sword, from the sleep
        Of its scabbard would leap,
  And conduct, with its point, every flash to the deep.

For ne'er shall the sons of Columbia be slaves . . ."

215

Mr. Thomas Paine had written many more stanzas, but
these two rang reverberant above me, while the commander of that vessel was not unmindful of their
message.

"And what may yo' be doin' alone in this corner o'
the Mediterranean Sea?" he asked.

The voice again was at the chorus of that famous
ditty:

"For ne'er shall the sons of Columbia be slaves . . ."

"Lieutenant —" I began, beginning to be disconcerted by the still wondering, silent faces of the sailors
encircling us, and only that song from above and the
slight roll of the ship to accompany it.

"Decatur," says he jauntily.

"Lieutenant Decatur, sir," I answered, "do you command this ketch?"

"Yes, Barbary Bo," he agreed, with a tolerant smile,
whereat all the men laughed heartily.

"Then," I concluded, flushing to the roots of my hair,
but remembering the importance of my mission and
indicating the crowd around us, "I'll be glad to tell you
all about myself, and more besides — after thanking you

for saving me — but it must be for your ears alone, sir."

Those were bold words I now uttered, not wholly uninspired, perhaps, by the words of that last song; but they were necessary, too — and I have always found naval folk ready to appreciate blunt frankness. Decatur's smile, so unlike Sidi Mahommed's, broadened.

"Yo' call runnin' yo' down savin' yo', lad?"

I nodded.

"Well, your story must be worth listenin' to. But don't you need some food first? I've a mite of time on my hands."

"I don't need food so bad but that I can wait," I assured him.

Instantly he waved a comprehensive arm, and the laxness of the surrounding sailors vanished as by magic: "Clear away, every man Jack of you!"

They melted, down hatches, round yards. He and I had that bit of deck to ourselves.

"Now!"

"Sir," I said, "the *Philadelphia* ran aground on October 31st in Tripoli harbor on a submerged rock-shelf not listed in the government map. She was captured by the enemy."

No smile now! My words made him mighty serious; yet he had news for me as well, the news that this portion of mine wasn't news at all to him:

"I know it. The *Vixen* sent out patrols and discovered as much. But how did a piratical-looking lad like you get to know it?"

"I was aboard the frigate, sir, when she struck and during the succeeding engagement."

"Member of her crew?"

"Captain Bainbridge's cabin boy."

"Our news was incomplete. Was everybody taken prisoner?"

"Yes, sir. No casualties. Only, you see, I've escaped at last."

"Alone?"

"Yes, sir."

His boyish face glowed appreciation. "How'd yo' manage it?"

Briefly I told him of the slaving toil of our men, of my service at the Kaya's and how I made my dash from

218

that shore now far out of sight behind the southern horizon.

"Splendid!" He banged his right fist into his left palm. "Just plum splendid pluck, that! — Bainbridge all right, eh? And Porter, and Gibbon — not too out of heart?"

"As right as could be expected in the circumstances, but not shouting 'Huzza.' I didn't run away from there to bring that word." So, at last, I revealed the plot against the *Vixen*.

"They'll have to travel far to find her," said Decatur grimly. "Johnnie Smith'd had held her there till doomsday, being a stickler o' the first class fo' orders, if he hadn't heard by chance o' the *Philadelphia's* fate. I expect by now all the seventeen States are buzzing with it. But o' cou'se, his duty was to take the intelligence to base an' not stay prowlin' around these dangerous waters. She's there yet, the *Vixen* is, and so I've been sent out fo' a li'l' job — a li'l' job that pleases me — us an' the *Siren*."

He pointed off the larboard bow. Standing toward us was a brig, its commander silhouetted distinct at the

219

taffrail looking out over the water: those square sails I had imagined from my rowboat had not after all been the material of desire or delirium.

"There's one thing more, sir," said I. "I've got Captain Bainbridge's report here with me, to give to Commodore Preble."

"Ah!" Decatur thrust out an eager, open-fingered hand. "I must have that right away."

My own fingers went to the spot where I had stowed the parchment. They were in the act of closing on it and bringing it out, when I was aware of some sudden fancy visibly affecting the Lieutenant; a stiffness that was more than formality fell upon him. I paused, wondering what it could mean.

"An' don't it occur to you," he said in his drawl, but somewhat portentously now, "since yo' have my name, me being commander o' this craft, I might be given yours? I'd like to know who the United States Navy has got to thank fo' a mighty good piece o' work."

"My name," I answered him promptly, "is Martin Rowntree."

I could never have dreamed that the mention of who I

was could produce an effect so startling on anybody. Changed a little a moment since, at this pronouncement the whole man changed completely — changed so quickly that I stood there paralyzed. Decatur's lithe frame hardened; his shoulders went back; his head went high; blood flooded his cheeks, and his eyes narrowed and hardened as if they believed themselves tricked.

"What's that?" he demanded. His gaze seemed to look right into me, until the whole man became as it were just two bright spots of eyes — one saw nothing else, and I looked, fascinated in my alarm. "Martin Rowntree? You say you are Martin Rowntree?"

"Why, yes," my tongue made answer.

"Ha! I was late in guessing it, but guess it I did. Why, are you so looney you don't know there's an order about yo' to every commander of every American vessel on the Mediterranean station, an' a spanking reward of a thousand dollars offered fo' the arrest o' the Cadiz thief. Pluck? Proud o' yo'? Your folks'll be as proud o' you as they'd be o' the man who stole the admiral's pig —".

"I didn't steal — I didn't steal anything," I fairly

221

shrieked.

"Very right and proper, but yo're to be apprehended on sight at any port where yo' put your nose, an' any port includes my vessel when yo're hauled aboard her. Our Consul, Mr. Wigglesworth, at Cadiz has laid a fo'mal charge against Martin Rowntree fo' robbin' and helpin' himself out o' the consular-safe!"

CHAPTER XVI

"BURN HER — AND MAKE GOOD
YOUR ESCAPE"

FROM that quarter wherein, aboard my rowboat, I had seen the clouds over unseen Africa gather, the weather was perceptibly thickening. A chill had come upon the air, and, far away to the south-ward, the waves slightly whitened. The ketch was running like a stag, but under her keel the water began to talk like a thing possessed.

A sailor advanced, squinting as some spray soused on to him.

"What's the rally for?" demanded Decatur.

"Gale comin', sir," said he; "that sirocco'll be on us in a jiffy."

"Get out!" The Lieutenant fairly barked it. "Spike your guns," which meant he would accept no interrupting till he'd finished with me.

He had not so much as looked at the fellow — only

223

made a quick gesture. But it was comprehensible enough to the sailor, who did not wait for a second order. He got out as if shot.

In my more vital and pressing exploits with Bainbridge and Bill Ray and the others, I had come at last to forget the chance of that false charge again assailing me. Oh, of course, I had sometimes feared that Ibrahim Bey was successful to some extent and had thrown on me the suspicion of his crime; yet time and events had dimmed his accusation, and I had thought it, after all, only for the exigencies of the moment. Besides, to dread disgrace is one affair; to meet it alive, accomplished, is another. A Rowntree charged with theft and treason, and that Rowntree I, who had put my life voluntarily in jeopardy to capture the real criminal: it almost put an end to my waning courage.

"It's a lie!" I cried out rebelliously. "It's a low lie!"

"It's a fo'mal charge, laid by a trusted employee of the Government," said Lieutenant Decatur solemnly: "Ahab — I don't cotton to his Yankee name; I confess; but he can't help his name or place o' birth — Ahab

Wigglesworth, as yo' must be well aware, is consul at Cadiz. Yo' were his consular-clerk if yo're Martin Rowntree." Decatur paused, then volleyed: "Yo' were his consular-clerk, weren't yo'?"

The world spun round me all which-way.

"It was the Vice Consul who did it," I tried to explain; "he came in while I was napping like a ninny, and he stole the gold — and whatever else was stolen: Ibrahim Bey — he was going under the name of Ventura Gonzales, but it was never his baptized name. He pretended he was a Spaniard, and Mr. Wigglesworth was just hoodwinked by him."

"My information is to the effect that this Señor Gonzales is on leave fo' personal business in Constantinople, and it was in his absence that yo' managed to do the stealin'."

"He came back! That night, and he's in Tripoli at this moment, and he's going to France as soon as he's led out the *Philadelphia* in search of the *Vixen!* Why, he's to be commander of her! And do you know for why?" Righteous anger was beginning to overcome in me a false shame for an offense of which I wasn't guilty.

"Because one of the things he stole from that safe — the chiefest thing — was a certain letter written by Secretary Madison to Yusuf's brother, who's the rightful heir to Tripoli's throne."

While every now and then the spray would rise up and crash down upon us and an extra wave would burst on deck with a smashing sound, I poured out my story of that portentous evening in Cadiz — of my pursuit through the city and across the Mountains of the Night under guidance of Silverio and his gypsies — of the scene upon the *Mastico* and Algeciras, and how I got to the *Philadelphia* and stowed-away aboard her — and what, finally, I saw and overheard in Tripoli. But Bainbridge had, when I first recounted it, doubted utterly the first part of my chronicle as a fabrication; it was an odd tale, and it is hard to tell even a true history convincingly once it has been ridiculed. Decatur shook his curly head as if he was only sorry for me as a craven liar.

"And, by your own showing, every one o' your witnesses are out o' reach. That's no manner of a successful falsehood, Barbary."

226

It was crushingly true that my witnesses were scattered to the four corners of the earth. I took another tack:

"Wouldn't I have stayed a slave in Tripoli — would I have ever tried to escape — would I have told you this about Captain Bainbridge — if I were a traitor to the United States?"

"Tut, tut. Yo' say yo'self that paper was worth something precious high to the big European powers. Weren't yo' mebby out lookin' fo' a French ship when I ran yo' down?"

"A French ship — out here, sir?"

"Why not? Bony'll be an emperor yet 'most befo' yo' can say Jack Robinson, and he's got his boats right nigh everywhere, these days."

I cared nothing about Napoleon's destiny, even if he could have himself made First Consul for life. "Then," I challenged the man facing me with his eyes still boring into my eyes, "search me for that letter."

"Its absence wouldn't prove your innocence." Decatur shrugged. He had, as his name implied, a lot of Gallic blood in him and a lot of retort always ready.

"Yo' might 'a' sold it to that fat Pasha — yo' bein' a bad business-man."

I hadn't guessed southern speech could sound so cold. I said:

"But I've got Captain Bainbridge's report, I tell you — he trusted me."

"How'd I know that? And if it's true, how'd I know yo' weren't playin' Bainbridge false? How'd I know yo' aren't a renegade come out here — the spy I thought first-off yo' were? An American boy'd who'd gone wrong would make a right likely spy for that herd o' heathen Tripolitans."

It was so much give-and-take I was near beside myself with confusion. Everything I had said or done seemed to add color to the theory of my shame! "Still," I weakly argued, "I have got that report."

"Then," said Lieutenant Decatur calmly, "give it to me."

A little light began to illuminate my darkness, and my anger flared up. "I don't know as I will, since you think so ill of me, sir. After all, it's not addressed to you: Captain Bainbridge addressed it to Commodore

Preble and nobody else."

One storm was advancing at a not far-distant canter along the waters, with the waves hissing and spuming and glimmering into brightness; another storm began to break on Decatur's face. "Commodore Preble's back at base. Here and now, I represent him."

But my only anchor was that report. It could be taken from me by force, only —

"It's addressed to the Commodore," said I, stubbornly, "and if you don't know things rightly about me, how can I be expected to know rightly that you represent the Commodore?"

Our eyes met and held a moment. I had something he wanted, on my side; on his was something that I meant to have: the chance to prove my innocence at whatever risk of his annoyance.

"But, boy," he stormed — himself only a boy — "I got to see Bainbridge's report! I have got to secure all the info'mation I can get!" Why, you will ask, didn't he summon his men and seize the paper? I asked myself the same question, greatly puzzled: its answer came later. "Can't yo'," he pursued in his confidential young way, "can't yo' guess why I am here? A few weeks ago, the *Vixen* captured this very ketch — it was the *Mastico* then, and Tripolitan; now we've made her American and renamed her the *Intrepid*. Well, she bein' that, and you bein' aboard her to stay whether yo're foe or friend, I'm free to tell yo' why I'm sent out in her." — He fumbled at a pocket — handed me a paper. "Look through this, since yo' know clerkin' — and therefore how to read."

Although my grasp was uncertain, and I marvelled at his letting me peruse it even if I must stay aboard the ketch, I read word-by-word his since historic orders from Commodore Preble:

"It is my order that you proceed to Tripoli in company with the *Siren*, Lieutenant Stewart, enter that harbor in the night, board the *Philadelphia*, burn her —"

"*Burn* her?" I gasped.

He nodded, lips set.

I read on:

" . . . Burn her and make good your retreat with the *Intrepid*, if possible, unless you can make her the means of destroying the enemy's vessels in the harbor, by converting her into a fire-ship for that purpose, and retreating in your boats and those of the *Siren*. You must take fixed ammunition and apparatus for the frigate's eighteen-pounders, and if you can, without risking too much, you may endeavor to make them the instruments of destruction to the shipping and Bashaw's castle. You will provide all the necessary combustibles for burning and destroying ships. The destruction of the *Philadelphia* is an object of great importance and I rely with confidence on your intrepidity and enterprise to effect it. Lieutenant Stewart will support you with the boats of the *Siren* and cover your retreat with that vessel. Be sure and set fire in the gun-room berths, cockpit, store-rooms forward and berths on the berth-deck. After the ship is well on fire, blow her bottom out."

"Yo' see," said Decatur in his soft drawl, "we'll make a navy for the United States of America yet, even if we have to blow the bottoms out of some of her ships to confound the enemy."

The words of the orders danced before my eyes. For

just that moment, horror at my own plight and marvel
at Decatur's action in showing them to me were alike
swallowed up by enthusiasm.

There I stood on the old *Mastico's* deck and under
the mottled, growling sky, all but disgraced, accused on
high authority of treasonable theft. A little while ago,
a mere moment since, indeed, despair had overcome me,
and yet, now, for one flying instant, honestly, in my
heart and consciousness nothing remained save love of
my country.

"Whatever you are," spoke up Decatur, always eye-
ing me closely, and putting back in his pocket the orders
I handed to him, "you are an American o' some sort, an'
yo' see I've been frank with yo'. Yo' declare yo're an
honest citizen; then prove it. That report o' Bainbridge's is addressed to Preble, o' cou'se, but Preble's
not here, and it belongs more to our country's cause at
large, and her necessity — and when the country's concerned, I say 'To Davy Jones's locker with regulations
and etiquette!'" — What had become of the man that
I had thought might be a dandy? He was become
intensity incarnate! — "I can take the paper from yo'

232

anyhow. The only question is: will yo' give it freely?"

Decatur was right. My duty to America stood above my duty to my personal reputation and my family's, and the false pride that seethed in me; and yet, knowing the secret of that invisible ink and believing I could use my knowledge at long last to my own advantage, I tried to dicker.

"What are you going to do with me?" I asked, as bold as brass. It might not matter to him, but it mattered a worldful to me.

"Do with yo'? he flashed, while the wind began to moan ominously overhead, "don't yo' see what I'm tryin' to do? I'm just givin' yo' an opportunity to have a few extenuatin' deeds advanced in your favor at the trial that'll take place over you in Spain, grantin' we get there. Meantime, there's a snug li'l' jail aboard the *Intrepid*, and I'm going to have yo' put into it."

This was worse than my plight when confronting Bainbridge on the *Philadelphia!* My fingers returned to the hiding-place of the report. With no further delay, I drew it out and held it toward him.

He snatched it — unfolded it, after breaking the

233

seal — glanced first at one side and then at the other.
I had thought there came an odd disappointment in his
expression when I made that surrender, but here it was
chased away by stupefaction, which a fierce anger replaced as he pounced at me. He had me instantly by
the shirt-collar; he shook me till I thought my head
must snap clean off my shoulders.

"What sort of a bad joke is this?" he vociferated.
"The paper's blank!"

The collar tore free, remaining in his clutch while I
fell plump against the rail. I saw a pair of sailors,
stopping their polishing to grin at me, but I pulled
myself together.

"The report's — written — in invisible ink," I gasped
from where I braced myself. For a last effort — the
dicker to which my course had been directed — I summoned all my breath. "What I'm going to ask you
sounds as if I were really a spy. I can't help that. You
don't know how to make that writing stand out, sir, but
I do — and it's a true paper: I swear it. If you happen
to be familiar with Captain Bainbridge's hand, you'll
recognize it there. But — but — I'll tell you the
secret only if you'll give me your promise to do the

thing I want."

Decatur's wrath halted in amazement. He regarded me sharply. "Eh?" he snorted. Then, "Of all the unmitigated cheek —"

I meant to hold to my decision for dear-life.

"Unless Ibrahim Bey — that is, Ventura Gonzales — is now aboard the *Philadelphia* getting her ready to sail, he's ashore somewhere in Tripoli," I concluded; "wherever he is, he's got the Secretary's letter on him, for he's not yet had chance to negotiate it to his liking — and as long as he's at large and not an American prisoner, I can't actually prove I'm not its thief."

"Well? Well?"

"Let me go with you, sir — to the frigate — and fight with you there. If he isn't aboard her then — well, when she's destroyed, let me go back to the city and be a slave to the pirates again, just so I can be near to that scoundrel and perhaps somehow get a chance to lay him by the heels. That's my proposal, sir — and if you don't agree to it, I'll never tell you how to read this report, never, never, never, no matter what you do to me; and you can't read it unless I tell you how! And I'm not afraid! I'm not afraid at all!"

235

CHAPTER XVII

"THE WATCHWORD'S 'PHILADELPHIA'!"

I DO not excuse myself. Here was a United States officer under orders to attempt a hazardous, most likely an impossible, adventure. He did indeed need all the information regarding Tripoli, its harbor and defenses and the idiosyncrasies of the captured frigate that he could get, and I knew that report, having seen a bit of it as Bainbridge wrote it, to contain much such matter: my duty as a citizen was to forget my personal honor. All I can say in defense is that I was ashamed of myself as soon as the last words of the proposal left my mouth. But what was I to say of the effect they had on Decatur? He burst out laughing!

He did more. I had thought he considered my touch contamination by now; to my amazement he seized hold of me — not in the least to punish me: he gave me a big, friendly hug.

"I was so afraid yo' wouldn't say it!" he rejoiced.

236

"Boy — boy, I've been tryin' to make yo' say it — wastin' valuable time — fo' I don't know how long! If this paper is in Bainbridge's hand — and o' cou'se it is — yo're no spy; and when yo' ask to fight with me and go back to slavery to scotch that Ibrahim-rapscallion, yo' prove — to me, leastways — that the Yankee Consul's charge against yo's a tale not fit even to tell to the marines! I couldn't bear to think it was anything mo', but, boy, I had to have proof!"

Imagine my amazement. Yet that was Stephen Decatur all over. What lawyers and landsharks call evidence meant nothing to him. He had a way of judging men by his own knowledge of human nature and, having made a test he believed to be successful, he stood by it against all the world:

"Yo' sho' will board that frigate with me an' have all the rest o' yo' heart's desire!"

I tried to speak — failed. But he ran on like a delighted child, which, in truth, this fire-eater often was:

"We must have our papers regular — must enter yo' on the roster o' the ship. Let's see: what'll we call yo'? Yo' own name's suspicious an' might get yo' into a

237

power o' trouble — an' me, too. I know! We'll set yo' down as 'Barbary Bo,' castaway — picked up on this date."

He did it, too. "Bo" was a term of friendship then coming into favor among mariners; as "Barbary Bo" I stand upon the *Intrepid's* roster in the Navy's records to this day.

Such was the fashion of my entering service under Decatur, and, although I never lost my respect and affection for Captain Bainbridge, I am bound to say that the Marylander's character appealed more strongly to my imagination. No sooner had I met his test, and he reached his decision, than I became a proper member with his crew, with a somewhat vague place, perhaps, but solid for all that and close attached to the person of the commander. What he called my "outlandish heathen clothes" were taken from me, as soon as I was fed, and replaced by a regular U.S. sailor's uniform. I felt more important than His Tripolital Majesty, Yusuf Pasha, son of the Prophet, Conqueror and Great!

That storm which had been brewing hit us before I was much more than reclothed, and held us veritable prisoners out at sea when we were all on fire to hurry to our rash enterprise. It gave me, too, aboard this ketch, a scorn for Moorish naval architecture and a high regard for the long-suffering Moors who were obliged to put up with it, not knowing its absurdities.

. We were seventy-three on the *Intrepid,* which had been originally the *Mastico:* the skipper, three full-fledged officers, a saw-bones, a lot of midshipmen, nine warrant officers, the gun-crew and a steward, thirty-four seamen — able and ordinary — our pilot, a sergeant, corporal and six marines; and we were mere herring in a barrel. There was but one cabin, and it was mighty small and shared by Decatur, the trio of other lieutenants, Jimmie Lawrence, later of "Don't-give-up-the-ship" fame, among them, and the surgeon, Dr. Herrmann, a Pensylvania-Dutchman and so hailing from my own State. The half-dozen middies and the pilot (who was that Italian I'd seen when I scrambled up over the side: a Sicilian named Catalano; he knew Tripoli's harbor inch by inch) occupied a platform laid on the water-casks, so confined below the deck that they could only barely manage to sit up. The marines made out in about the same way, and, as for the sailors, they slept on the casks in the hold.

Well, as was to be foreseen, the provisions had gone bad, the Moors had left no end of lice and other vermin behind them, and that storm held us up for a good thirty-six hours. I will leave you to guess whether even an arrant coward wouldn't have preferred rushing to our tough attack on the *Philadelphia*.

"Do you think the frigate will have come out in the meantime?" I asked of one of the under-officers, Jonothan Thorn, who had heard my story, as for that matter, most had.

"Don't you bother," said he. "These Moors have already guessed that you made your escape by water, and they think you have warned the *Vixen*. Besides, they never do anything on time."

It was hard waiting, and we lost touch with the *Siren* somehow during the worse of the blow, the Mediterranean acting up more than anybody would have given that blue lake credit for being able to do. However, all things must come to an end sometime: that gale finished at last. The night fell fine, with only a light wind. I

went out on deck, and wriggled my way through to a
place near our commander, who had taken station in the
prow.

"We'll stand right in toward shore," he told his sailing-master.

That officer saluted. "And not wait for our consort,
sir?" he asked doubtfully.

"Not here," says Decatur very sharp. "But," he
added with more consideration, "we'll heave the drags
out, so's we aren't too rapid about it."

Stars hung over the rigging. For a long time, everything else was purple darkness, and of course we showed
no light. A little after eight P.M., some twinklings appeared off our larboard bow: lamps on land. The pilot,
Catalano, ran forward.

"We're two a-mile east o' de harbor-mout'," he announced.

And it was plain that we were unobserved — unexpected. "Lay to," ordered Decatur.

We dropped anchor. The chains had been greased
with the utmost attention, and that operation could not
have been accomplished with less commotion. We were
to remain here, according to plan, until four-bells —

only they wouldn't ring! — when certain small-boats from the *Siren* were to join us.

But Decatur wouldn't attend a second longer than the schedule called for. He was all for things on time, and there was no sign of the *Siren* on the stroke of ten — much less of any boats from her. Waiting, we watched the young moon rise.

"We'll proceed without 'em," decided our skipper, at length.

He peered along the empty vastness of the sea — no sign of our consort.

Somewhere in toward shore, in the blackness between those dancing shore-lights and the deck whereon I stood, lay the *Philadelphia* with, only too likely, traitorous Ibrahim Bey aboard her as her commander — somewhere ahead there, most assuredly he was, and he held my honor in a pocket. But I was now being given my chance to go after him: I could have cheered!

Long before ever I came to the ketch, every man-jack of her crew that was to board the frigate had been thoroughly drilled in his rôle; but now Decatur ordered them around him and, under the waxing moonshine, repeated his carefully thought-out instructions. Those brave lads made me jump when they appeared, for all the world like black pirates themselves, for hardly a one but was disguised in Moorish clothes.

The pilot was perhaps the most villainous-looking of them all.

"Catalano," said the commander, speaking in as common-place a manner as if he were commenting on the weather to a friend met in his home-town of Philadelphia, "if we're hailed, don' yo' forget we're the *Transfer*, the vessel that the Pasha lately bought in Malta an' that he's expectin' yere. We'll just drift in an' then man the longboat when I say to."

"Yes, sir," grinned the pilot: it was an uncanny grin in the moonlight.

"As fo' yo' other men, yo' aren't to use yo' firearms unless it's absolutely necessary, fo' Captain Bainbridge's report shows the frigate lies in easy range o' those pesky forts. We'll take the spar-deck first — next, the gun-deck — an' then yo'll divide in parties, accordin' to original instructions, with the combustibles fo' the rest o' yo' work. This moon won't be much help or much hindrance, so we'll need a watchword: the watchword's '*Philadelphia.*'"

CHAPTER XVIII

IN THE COCKPIT

THROUGH the faintly silver moonlight, we drifted in like a ghost-ship, blurred against the sky. We drifted so slowly, so silently, that I thought we should never arrive.

Decatur was now repeating his former instructions to the various officers that he had appointed to command those parties into which he had ordained that the boarders were eventually to divide.

"Midshipman Row and Izard!"

"Yes, sir." — They saluted.

"Yo're with me an' yo' fifteen men — to hold the spar-deck. — Lieutenant Lawrence?"

"Yes, sir."

"Yo', with Laws and Macdonough an' yo' ten men'll take care o' the berth-deck an' the staterooms. Midshipman Davies with yo' men, yo're fo' wardroom an' steerage. Morris, the cockpit an' the after-staterooms

244

are yo' care, as we arranged befo'. Thorn an' the doctor will stay aboard here an' hold the ketch against all comers, with yo' men, fo' our return an' escape — be ready to set sail at a moment's notice."

He had finished. I risked a question:

"And me, sir?"

He smiled — I could see it.

"Go with Morris, Barbary Bo," said Decatur. "That's what you're after, an' I know yo' want to prove yo'self by cou'tin' dange': all right, it's Morris who's to do the actual blowin' up o' the *Philadelphia*."

That round-faced middy heard and grinned at me, and I went up to him. He was near of my own age, blond and lithe, and no nonsense about him.

"You don't mind having me?"

"Glad," says he, looking at me straight, as he wrung my hand.

So we of the boarding-party grouped ourselves at the longboat-station while our ketch, the favoring wind astern, moved gradually shoreward under the stars and the steadily climbing moon. Its pale rays revealed us to to one another — eager young fellows and tars with set faces — it showed more and more distinctly those Moorish costumes awkwardly worn — glinted on the cutlasses that were served out to us and the fire-bombs distributed to Morris and his men.

"Cover those blades!"

Here now, ahead, towered the city, a phantom-city, as ghost-like as we ourselves had been, rising white above the waters' polished ebony. Across from it were ranged the forts. I was beginning to fear that the light must surely too soon discover us to our enemies when a sailor at last whispered:

"There she lies!"

True enough — here, a tall, dark shape, appeared what we were seeking: the *Philadelphia*, dead across our bows, a bare two hundred yards away. She had never left port, and by the torches of the men still at work aboard her, I knew her instantly. She lay pretty well out, top-masts housed, lower arms on gunwales; she had, of course, been completely repaired: she must be well manned and carry at the least forty guns, whereas our miserable sixty-ton ketch could boast of no more than four small cannon and was now arrived within range of the pitiless shore-batteries.

Somebody hailed us, but not exigently. Nevertheless, my heart rode to my mouth. That Sicilian pilot of ours replied, his clear voice ringing, that we were the *Transfer*, expected by the Pasha. He had no sooner spoken the words than the wind shifted. It blew from shore and left us at rest abeam and about sixty feet from the frigate.

Came Decatur's low voice:

"Boats — boats! *Now!*"

We all tumbled overside — all of us that were designated to go, sorry for those condemned to remain. Along with the rest, I went, close after Midshipman Morris. Whispers — cautions — muffled oars, now needlessly muffled.

Another hail reached us — this time incredulous. But we had already bumped against the *Philadelphia's* hull. A bare instant later, by the skilfully uptossed ladders we were swarming aboard. Every man was following his leader, and every leader knew exactly what he had to do.

Even as we struck deck, cries resounded, and the

scurrying of bare feet from the Moors still at work there. — Then was hurled, with terrifying impetus, a pell-mell rush at us as the crew, thus warned, scampered out from below.

Yet never, I suppose, has such an operation been carried through with less clámor. Only cutlasses were used at first — no yelping firearms. The forts, even the neighboring ships, for some time remained in ignorance of what was happening, and our immediate foes, being utterly astounded, had nothing except their native knives at hand.

The two parties met with a tremendous impact. Blades rose and fell. The Moors closed with our front rank, thrusting murderously. Yankees clubbed pistols and used leaden fists. I, hacking blade in hand, struck from the side of Morris with his gang behind him, while before us there retreated backward, still farther backward, an ugly black row of Tripolitans. Many a face I saw then that I had observed ashore during the days of my incarceration, but not the face that, now, I most of all sought — and yet I was more and more convinced that Ibrahim Bey must be somewhere aboard this boat.

248

"Stations!"

Decatur's voice rang out fearless. He was only a little distant from us.

Morris turned. "But, sir, if we could save this craft?" he cried; after all, she was our ship. "If we can cut her out?"

Our leader was adamant. "Do your work!"

That deck-fight was all going our way. An open hatch gaped before the blond middy.

"Come on!" he shouted — and plunged into it.

I plunged after him. After me plunged the rest of our particular party.

Down we went, I, giving the lead as a former member of the frigate's crew and familiar with her, but Morris pressing close behind. Some of the fellows now bore torches: they illuminated a little this descent into the bowels of the ship and set weird shadows prancing. Far under the water-line, we traversed, running, a passage with several staterooms opening off it, which I knew well. Their doors were all closed — and, at the extremity of this corridor, we confronted a heavy portal.

"That's it," said I. "The cockpit's on the farther

249

side of this door."

Against it Morris charged.

Shut!

He assumed it locked. Our gang pressed on from the rear, only waiting orders.

"Wait!"

With his bare knuckles, he began to hammer at it, madly. He even tried to force it with his shoulder.

Were it properly fastened, one man working alone could never have prevailed against it, though, to be sure, our massed force would have smashed the barrier in no time. To me, however, it occurred that Morris was losing his head. He had not yet tried the knob.

Tucking my cutlass into my belt, I reached around him and turned it — the door leaped open and snapped backward; at the instant, it sent flying in our direction an innocent key from the inside of the lock, which rattled to rest on the passage-floor as we poured through.

We were in the cockpit, the lot of us. It was a narrow place with cots for the reception of wounded during an action; Dr. Cowdery's instrument-case hung against the farther wall, untouched since the days when the

250

Philadelphia was truly American. Aft, one other door gave, as I knew, upon what had been the surgeon's cabin; as we rushed into the main compartment, I seemed to see that door closing, and there was jerked after it the form of a hand that seemed familiar.

"Mr. Morris —" I began.

He did not hear me. "Now then — to work!" he gasped, still pausing from that unnecessary struggle preceding our easy entrance.

Well, I made a rash decision: Here waited — unless I was greatly mistaken — something that had to be done and was best done alone. The advice of Bill Ray returned to me:

"Do what you have got to do — and do it as neat as pie; that's the secret of a happy life for a mariner."

All right, I myself, unaided, would make the capture that must rehabilitate me. I hardly listened as Morris repeated his ringing order: "To work!"

His party's task was hazardous — fatal, if speed failed. We were come here to start the fires that would blow the bottom out of this vessel, which done, we — beating our artificial volcano in a life-and-death race —

must get back on deck, rejoin our companions, and all return to the *Intrepid* ere the neighboring vessels discovered our identity. We worked with an insane, yet well-directed, fury; our fellows had been carefully rehearsed by Decatur: each knew and perfectly performed his rôle. The explosives were spread; from them, slow matches were laid to the entrance to the main door.

It was all a mere matter of five minutes. Morris himself it was who applied a torch. From three separate sources, smoke began slowly to fill the cockpit; from three separate starting-points, worms of fire wriggled toward the piles of explosives heaped in the centre of the cabin.

"On deck, everybody — and be lively about it!" shouted our leader.

The midshipman drew away for all to precede him, and they tore out, I with them. But I had not in the least forgotten my desperate purpose. The man with torches led the van; in the rear gloom, I stood aside against the wall and let unheeding Morris pass me.

Then I wheeled about. If I hurried, there might be

still time to accomplish what I wished. Although my fellows were remounting toward the deck, I reëntered the cockpit.

It was now completely full of smoke — smoke without actual fire. Its only lights were those which came from the sputtering slow-matches — none too slow and all too close to their deadly destination. Still, I could see well — and I saw, as I had expected, the door of that inner cabin opening.

Pallid from fear and framed by the rising gray fumes, here gazed at me, across that heap of mortal bombs, the once swarthy face of Ventura Gonzales — Ibrahim Bey.

253

CHAPTER XIX

THE DEATH–TRAP

YES, unmistakably here he was. Appointed to command this frigate when she put out to sea, here had he hidden — the cowardly bully! — when he realized we were boarding her. Hence, too, he hoped for escape between the moment when we left her and that at which she fell in pieces to the bottom of Tripoli's harbor. My man at last! I swung up my cutlass.

"Surrender!" I yelled, and I could hear the jangle of my voice, high and strained. "There's not a moment to lose. I need but leave you here, Ventura Gonzales, and you're a dead man!"

Only his face had I so far seen, thrust through that opening — black eyes wide, yellow fangs bared in horror. But now, of a sudden, it all altered. An arm darted around that half-opened door — and it levelled a pistol against which, at this distance, my poor sword-blade was entirely helpless.

"Drop your sabre!" he commanded.

He had me. What else could I do. Slowly, I dropped it.

Then, nimble as a collie-pup, that fellow vaulted into the cockpit. He leaped over the heap of explosives — leaped clean over them — threaded a path between the fires chasing now toward that fatal pyre and, thrusting his pistol trimly between my eyes, took me by the collar.

With the going-and-coming heat of his breath against my face, the obscene leer of his narrow eyes, the chill of those claws against the base of my neck, I was ready to collapse.

"Now," says he, "it's I, young rapscallion, who goes and you who will stay — and they'll report afterwards that you perished rather than be proved a thief and a traitor."

I think he overplayed, as card-folk say, his hand. Here we stood, the pair of us, beside a mound of explosives toward which those glow-worm fires moved with increasing vigor. There was no light where we were save the lights of approaching destruction; there was no air except the acrid air of burning powder which, ever as our lungs rejected it, we knew to be the threat ultimate. His only hope was to get clear of the cockpit before its fires ran their course — and my only hope was his. I could not stamp out those sputtering matches — he would not.

And yet, just because he threatened me with such a gigantic injustice, I found at least the courage requisite to force him to die with me. As he had held to my collar, so I took quick hold of his.

"Unless you shoot me first," I vowed, "we shall die here together."

I had, of course, been half mad. Murder he had held over my head — murder was his very trade. He laughed. "No sooner said than done!" he chortled — and I saw his narrow index-finger curling against the trigger of his pistol.

Time is a fiction. It is what our emotions make it. An instant may become an hour — an hour an instant. While Ibrahim Bey made ready to shoot, all the story of my life passed before me. I saw my boyhood on the banks of the Susquehanna — I saw my school — I saw my father, his face solemn but kindly, giving directions of life — I saw, clearest of all, my long-dead mother's face. I saw —

But now what I saw was no more vision. Instead, it was a far less credible reality. The closed door to the passage was immediately behind me; I had leaned against it so heavily that I near fell as it burst open — and what I actually beheld was somebody brushing by me, who covered with a pistol Ventura Gonzales just as that Turk now covered me.

"Come along!"

It was Silverio, the gypsy. He was in Moorish garb, but there was no more doubt of his identity possible than when I had observed him in the palace of the Pasha. Hoop-earrings — beak nose — even the oily, ingratiating smile was then exactly as it had been when first we had made acquaintance on the road, at the foot of the Mountains of the Night.

And "Come along," says he again, "for I won't hesitate to murder you rather than stay here and die myself like a rat."

To prove that he meant it, his talons fastened so quick and so tight around the Turk's throat that Ventura's tongue shot out . . .

Ibrahim Bey must either die or give up, and he wasn't the kind of man to choose heroic extinction. He came to us like a baa-lamb — but like a lamb in something of a hurry!

"It is very simple," explained Silverio as we rushed along the corridor — for no amount of running could disturb his fluent speech. "I am all that I told you — only more. Hamet, the true heir of Tripoli's throne, is exiled in Derne. He was warned of that letter from your Secretary of State and sent me, an unsuspected Romany, to get it. I came to Gibraltar, because the Algeciras officers were not friendly —" he grinned sheeplishly: "perhaps they remembered me as a smuggler."

"But," I protested, "Gonzales preceded me. Why did you not —"

"I passed the fellow, unsuspecting; then I met you. Well, I had often enough played the spy in Tripoli: who better than me with my glib tongue of many languages.

But to cross palms with gold and — But Algeciras was forbidden me — and not a boat to this port from Estopona." Then he became again the cunning, covetous creature that I had known of old. "I have read something of a reward. The young *señor* gave me, outside Algeciras, just enough for two breakfasts and one scanty dinner — after all my kindness to him. Will he now be pleased to testify in my behalf for what his Consul at Cadiz has offered?"

The last of our men were already dropping into their boats, helter-skelter, for time counted now. We shoved Gonzales, alias Ibrahim Bey, alias Heaven knows what else beside, into the final one and jumped in after him.

From the doomed frigate, her Moorish crew, now that the Americans no longer held them at bay, dived into the sea and swam, bare legs and black heads bobbing, for shore. The forts had detected us at last; their crazy guns were booming ominously, and the other vessels were setting up sail with panic haste; but we reached the *Intrepid* according to plan and soon showed all pursuers a clean pair of heels.

A burst of flame rose straight up. A horrible, rending roar beat our ear-drums. The *Philadelphia* split in halves and sank before our eyes.

Thus was our country's honor avenged. What the great English Admiral Nelson later called "the most bold and daring act of the age" had taken place in less than half an hour, and our only misfortune was one seaman slightly wounded.

It was many a day before I could get the chance to give back his precious Geneva to Captain Bainbridge, at last released, or ever I could see Lieutenant Porter or Bill Ray and those other brave fellows again. As for Wilson and his cronies, having turned more or less bona fide Mohammedans, they were obliged to stay in Tripoli and bow to their religion. But I hadn't been aboard the speeding ketch for five minutes before I claimed Decatur's attention — and got it.

"Sir," said I, saluting — and standing very straight, "here's a prisoner: the late American Vice Consul at Cadiz — and if you will take off his shirt, you will find he carries a certain stolen paper."

The gold? What was borne away had long since slid

260

through Ibrahim Bey's slippery fingers, but at least it wasn't needed any more to pay tribute to the Barbary States! The reward? It eventually went to Silverio, the gypsy, as he had earnestly hoped, though he did somewhat grudgingly offer to share it with me. What mattered to me most, however, was that, with Stephen Decatur himself to back me, I established my endangered reputation with the authorities, my honor with my father (who had never doubted it), and won myself a commission in the U.S. Navy.

THE END

9 781015 025950